THE FUTURE OF THE ORGANIZATION
OF AMERICAN STATES

The FUTURE *of the* ORGANIZATION *of* AMERICAN STATES

ESSAYS BY

Viron P. Vaky
Heraldo Muñoz

The Twentieth Century Fund Press • New York City • 1993

The Twentieth Century Fund is a research foundation undertaking timely analyses of economic, political, and social issues. Not-for-profit and nonpartisan, the Fund was founded in 1919 and endowed by Edward A. Filene.

Library of Congress Cataloging-in-Publication Data

Vaky, Viron P.
   The future of the Organization of American States / by Heraldo Muñoz, Viron P. Vaky.
   p. cm.
   Includes index.
   ISBN 0-87078-348-3 : $9.95
   1. Organization of American States. I. Muñoz, Heraldo
II. Title.
F1402.M86 1993
341.24'5—dc20

OCLC: 28707835

93–31243
CIP

Cover Design and Illustration: Claude Goodwin
Manufactured in the United States of America.
Copyright © 1993 by the Twentieth Century Fund, Inc.

FOREWORD

Almost every aspect of American foreign policy has been subject to reexamination in the aftermath of the cold war. The struggle with the Soviet Union was a prism that shaped our perceptions of all international relationships, including those with the nations closest to us. Indeed, the mix of U.S. interests and goals in the Western Hemisphere probably has changed not only in terms of what it was before the break up of the Soviet Union, but also in terms of what it was during any previous period. As a practical matter, in this hemisphere the United States has long been what it now is globally, the sole superpower. But its military preponderance did not then mean and does not now mean that it can enforce its will in every situation. Nor does the term superpower turn out to mean that the United States can expect to regain (or sustain, depending on whose numbers you use) its overwhelming global economic preeminence.

In one sense, the cold war simplified policymaking, providing a universal test for judging friends and presumptive enemies, a "higher morality" about when to act and when to tolerate. In retrospect, this purity of purpose gave ready form to the otherwise immensely complicated task of global leadership inherited by the nation after World War II. In the Americas, the one area of long-term U.S. hegemony, it provided a justification for continuing an ancient habit of sporadic intervention in the internal affairs of neighboring states. Yet, if anything, the traditional practice of interference was softened by the need to win friends in the fight to contain communism and by the competing demands of the extensive network of American alliances.

Today, we are at an early stage of discovering what sort of role the United States will play in the region and, more specifically, in its multinational organizations in the post-cold war era. Indeed, we are in the process of learning just what such organizations can and cannot do in a world without the certainties of the cold war. In some cases—NATO is the obvious example—it is not at all clear that a given institution will survive in anything like its previous form. In others—the United Nations clearly comes to mind—a broadened and heightened role in the world is already under way, likely to continue, and perhaps even to expand. And in still others—such as the Organization of American States (OAS)—it may be that the sort of partnership often described in rhetoric now has a chance to become a reality.

In this still evolving situation, U.S. foreign policy goals and methods necessarily seem unsettled, a work in progress even in the region that is its own backyard. To help explore such questions of present and future policy, the Twentieth Century Fund commissioned a series of studies about the U.S. role in a variety of international organizations. For example, this volume on the OAS is a part of a series of publications on U.S.-Latin American relations that the Fund is sponsoring.

This fall, the Fund, which co-sponsored a conference on the future of the United Nations with Wilton Park, an arm of the British Foreign Ministry, will release an edited volume by the conference participants that focuses on U.S. policy at the United Nations, and Max Jakobson's *The United Nations in the 1990s: A Second Chance?*, a Twentieth Century Fund Book, will be published by UNITAR. In addition, Jerome Levinson's study of the U.S. role in multilateral financial institutions will be published by The Twentieth Century Fund Press later this year.

This volume focuses on the special challenges facing the OAS in the post-cold war era. Its authors identify new opportunities for the institution to extend its reach beyond the limited and often unpopular role it played in the past. But they explain, as well, the significant limitations it still faces: Viron P. Vaky, a former U.S. ambassador to several Latin American countries, examines structural and procedural issues and offers suggestions for improving the effectiveness of the OAS in hemispheric relations. Heraldo Muñoz, Chile's ambassador to the OAS, provides an insider's perspective as he discusses the evolving mission of the OAS and focuses on what he sees as its central task: the defense of democracy in the region.

The Trustees of the Twentieth Century Fund appreciate the efforts of both authors to explore the changing terrain of U.S. foreign policy in the Western Hemisphere.

Richard C. Leone, *President*
The Twentieth Century Fund
August 1993

CONTENTS

THE ORGANIZATION OF AMERICAN STATES AND MULTILATERALISM IN THE AMERICAS

VIRON P. VAKY

INTRODUCTION

The changes in international politics flowing from "1989 and all that"[1] have altered the conceptual bases of inter-American relations. The cold war security motivation of U.S. hemisphere policy has disappeared, and with it the traditional perceptions of external threat. Conventional security/military questions have been displaced by issues of political economy as the primary context of hemisphere relations. A regionwide consensus on the validity of democratic political systems and free market economic models has created new common ground between the United States and Latin America, as well as shared approaches to problems of equal concern to both. Both the United States and Latin American countries are demonstrating a pragmatic awareness of the value of a cooperative relationship with each other. For one of the rare times in the region's history, the various national interests appear to converge substantially more than they conflict.

A collegial atmosphere has developed over the past three years, which among other things has sparked a revival of member states' interest in the Organization of American States (OAS) as an instrument for dealing with common problems. Beginning in 1990, the nations of the hemisphere drew up an extensive agenda for the organization, based on the assumptions of shared values, similar political systems, growing economic interdependence, and common concerns. As the member states move to translate their rhetoric into action, however, they find themselves confronted with all the thorny dilemmas inherent in coping with interdependence in a world of sovereign states. Sensitive, even unprecedented, questions of sovereignty and nonintervention have been posed with respect to a whole series of issues that are as much domestic as international in nature.

3

All this raises a basic question that is the central concern of this paper: Can the member states respond creatively to the challenges and opportunities presented by the "new world order" and thus convert the OAS into an effective agent of regional governance and "regime-building"?[2] Or will the organization be so constrained by the unilateral actions and varying interests of the member states as to be unable to adapt its tasks, goals, and structures to the new demands placed upon it, and so end up as marginal and redundant?

To examine these questions first requires a look at the new global setting created by the profound events that have taken place in recent years. Some of the considerations involved in pursuing a generic strategy of multilateralism will then be appraised. An examination of the OAS experience follows, surveying the organization's principal substantive activity, with particular focus on the commitment to promote and defend democracy since that issue is currently the center of its attention. After then analyzing the major structural questions and operational dilemmas confronting the OAS, the paper will draw some conclusions regarding its role and future.

CHAPTER I

THE INTERNATIONAL SETTING

The cold war was the central organizing principle that defined and dominated international relations for almost fifty years, and its end left a conceptual vacuum in foreign policy strategies. With no similar organizing principle likely to emerge in the 1990s, policymakers are struggling to define some new framework for making sense out of the current realities of world politics, and to elucidate some vision (a "new world order") to guide efforts to manage and shape them.

Complicating this effort are the contradictory dynamics unleashed by two major international developments: the sudden collapse of the Soviet empire and the dramatic increase in global interdependence. On the one hand, the integrating and unifying effect of science and technology, instantaneous communications, a world trading system, the global nature of the financial system, and the internationalization of manufacturing have all changed the way nations interact and what they can expect to achieve by themselves. No major issue confronting nations today—physical security, regional conflict, proliferation of weapons systems, economic and financial problems, environmental questions, migrations and refugees, humanitarian and human rights questions—can satisfactorily be dealt with unilaterally or by the traditional principle of "self-help." Indeed, cognizance of this heightened global interdependence changes the way nations establish their foreign policy priorities, and underscores the increasingly limited ability and usefulness of trying to exercise national autonomy in the world system today.

On the other hand, the end of the East-West conflict released long-suppressed yet deep-seated, centrifugal forces of nationalism, ethnicity, religious drives, and different cultural and nationalist aspirations and perspectives. The world system is thus caught between simultaneous "forces of integration and fragmentation," to use John Lewis Gaddis's phrase.[1]

The initial surge of optimism that accompanied the end of the cold war and the call for a "new world order" has since given way to rising uncertainty and confusion. The events that fill the headlines today— ethnic "cleansing," the breakup of nations, refugee flows, famines, internal insurgencies, social unrest, and trade wars—are all reminiscent of old-fashioned power politics. Some suggest that the traditional "realist" paradigm of an anarchic system in which sovereign nation-states compete in zero-sum terms has not basically changed, and that nations should therefore return to traditional "balance of power" strategies to protect their interests.[2]

Yet the patterns and structures of international politics do in fact now differ in critical and fundamental ways from the classical models.[3] The nation-state continues to be the paramount political entity; but alongside it are new networks of powerful nonstate actors, of transnational private and public links, and of global economic alliances, all of which add up to coexistence among different systems of interactions in a multicentric, "layer cake" kind of world.

Whatever the theoretical arguments, it is fair to conclude that the tensions, contradictions, and conflicts inherent in the current state of international affairs are unlikely to be adequately managed unless nations develop the methods, procedures, and institutional links for collective problem-solving and cooperation. If they do not, old-fashioned power politics may remain by default the only "game in town," however inadequate and ill-suited it may be to the new circumstances.[4] The result in that case would almost surely be a chaotic—and dangerous—world marked by international rivalries and resentments, ethnic and religious turmoil, civil wars, poverty and economic inequities, population pressures and huge migratory movements, and the prospect for environmental and ecological disasters.

Efforts to develop effective international organizations are, in short, a matter of the sheerest prudence.

States can act on collective interests without institutions or formal organization, of course, but institutionalization can facilitate collaboration and make it more reliable and stable than under ad hoc arrangements. Institutionalization encourages a longer-term view of problems and establishes a stable framework and infrastructure for on-going cooperation. Organizations can also enhance cooperation by providing information that would otherwise be unavailable or difficult for individual governments to collect. Finally, a formal grouping can reduce duplication and offer economies of scale, resulting in lower costs for providing infrastructure, monitoring, and staffing in comparison with ad hoc functional arrangements.

International organizations, ad hoc collective ventures, and bilateral relations are not mutually exclusive spheres; nations use eclectic mixes of channels and strategies as their interests dictate. The fundamental dilemma of multilateralism embedded in the heart of every collective endeavor, however, is the tension between sovereignty and interdependence. The problem of how to create and maintain collective rules and norms in a world still composed of sovereign states has never been completely resolved. Generally, nations have found it easier to come to terms with this problem when the objectives of collective action are concrete, technical in nature, and clearly circumscribed. The consequences of not collectively dealing with such matters as AIDS, communication standards, or air safety are so clear-cut, after all, that even the most self-interested citizens cannot ignore them. When it comes to broad political questions, however, such as collective security, defending human rights, promoting democracy, or self-determination, the adjustment of national interests to external norms and standards becomes difficult and delicate.

The United States is currently caught up in a national debate over what its role and purpose in the world should be, and the foreign policy strategies it ought to adopt as a consequence. Multilateralism is suspect to some Americans on the grounds that it interferes with the free pursuit of national interests, hinders the exercise of real power, and gratuitously forfeits national freedom of action.[5] These arguments were more persuasive when world politics were governed by the bilateral superpower struggle. They are inadequate in the post-cold war world. In response to changed circumstances, the Bush administration, despite exceptions such as the invasion of Panama, diverged from its predecessor's unilateralism and increasingly emphasized collective strategies and problem solving as its term progressed. The Clinton administration appears to be even more intent on following a systematic multilateral strategy, which the U.S. Ambassador to the UN has described as "assertive multilateralism." The debate, nevertheless, remains inconclusive with the multilateralists besieged, on the one side, by the "only superpower left" school advocating U.S. leadership and management of the new world order, and, on the other, by those advocating an essentially inward-looking strategy concentrating only on our own narrowly defined self-interests and stressing self-reliance.[6]

The recent transformations in global security and economic relations have subtly but significantly improved the prospects for resolving the sovereignty/interdependence dichotomy. As Professor James Rosenau has observed, the dilemma for states today is how to maintain autonomy in an interdependent world, as distinguished from the old order's question of whether or not to comply with collective norms in a system of completely independent nation states:

> The world has become too complex and dynamic for independence to satisfy needs and wants. Instead, there is widespread recognition at the ideational level that needs and wants have to be sought through reciprocal arrangements with others, that it is not contradictory to maintain both autonomous and interdependent relationships in the global system.[7]

A related question for diplomacy is how to minimize the tension between globalism and regionalism. What is the role and purpose of a regional entity like the OAS at a time when the United Nations is extending its mandate? The relationship between the UN and the OAS is discussed in more detail later; but, as a general proposition, there is no necessary or inevitable contradiction between regional and global activity. Rather, great virtue is attached to the notion of "subsidiarity," meaning in a universal system problems are best dealt with at the most local level possible.

With the removal of the restraints imposed by the cold war's global geopolitical framework, regional organizations and regimes have become more active and more important, discovering that many of the problems of today's world are best dealt with in a regional context. Regional and even subregional entities can be valuable for the purpose of carrying out certain tasks because they often better understand the way programs and problems present themselves locally. Because the membership of a regional organization is more homogeneous than that of the UN, it can provide greater cohesion in terms of shared values, interests, and experience. That improves the prospect for consensus and action. Regional initiatives may also be the only way to make progress on problems for which global action is slow, difficult, or stalemated. They can become the "point of the spear" in getting broader undertakings started.

The advantages, limitations, and tensions of multilateralism apply with special relevance to the OAS.

CHAPTER 2

THE WESTERN HEMISPHERE EXPERIENCE

The inter-American system,[1] with its formal and informal institutions, processes, and patterns, is the oldest and most elaborate regional governance system in the world. Tracing its lineage to the First International Conference of American States held in Washington from November 1889 to April 1890, the system has now passed its centennial. That first conference, convened by Secretary of State James Blaine, established the International Union of American Republics to promote commercial relations among the nations of the hemisphere, with the Commercial Bureau of the American Republics—later to become the Pan American Union—as its permanent secretariat.[2]

The system's modern institutional structure, however, dates from the creation of the Organization of American States in 1948. The establishment of the OAS was essentially a regional response to the broader initiatives then under way to create new international institutions and a new international order in the wake of the world war that had just ended. At the United Nations Conference on International Organization in San Francisco in 1945, it was the Latin American nations, representing close to half of the states attending, that insisted on the incorporation of provisions into the UN Charter that would allow for the maintenance of regional inter-American machinery.[3] The OAS Charter was, in effect, an expression of the member states' desire to codify the purposes and objectives of hemispheric cooperation and to institutionalize the conflict-resolution and collective security procedures adopted in the Americas before and during the war.[4] The substance of the Charter and accompanying treaties represented an implicit "bargain": in return for U.S. nonintervention in their internal affairs, the Latin American countries would support the United States internationally and accept collective responsibility for security in the hemisphere.[5]

From 1948 to the mid-1960s, the OAS chalked up a respectable record of accomplishments. Some forty disputes were resolved by OAS machinery in the first twenty years.[6] In the late fifties and early sixties, the member states expanded the focus of the organization to include economic and social development. The creation of the Inter-American Development Bank and the establishment of the OAS technical assistance programs (described further below) date from this period. The major stimulus for expanding OAS activities in the economic and social area, however, was the call by President John Kennedy in 1961 for an alliance of the region's nations to overcome the economic and social problems of underdevelopment, with the specific aim of strengthening the forces of democracy. In August 1961, the member countries adopted the Charter of Punta del Este, which formally established the Alliance for Progress, set development goals, and specified commitments.

To implement the Alliance, the OAS established in 1963 a special committee, the Inter-American Committee for the Alliance for Progress (CIAP), composed of seven members (the United States and six others chosen by the Latin American countries) and a large technical secretariat, to carry out annual reviews of national and regional development plans for the purpose of providing recommendations and guidelines for aid donors and the recipients themselves. The annual reviews provided a very useful forum in which donor representatives could explore with recipient country economic officials the issues confronting the country and its plans for dealing with them. The extensive growth within the region of trained professionals and institutional resources capable of drawing up and executing economic and social development plans proved to be a particularly useful by-product of the annual review process.[7]

The Inter-American Commission on Human Rights (IACHR) was established in 1959. In 1969, the American Convention on Human Rights was signed, replacing the earlier, nonbinding American Declaration of the Rights and Duties of Man, which had been promulgated in 1948 at the time the OAS Charter was adopted. The number of ratifying countries needed to bring the Convention into effect was not reached until July 18, 1978. The Inter-American Court on Human Rights was established by the terms of the Convention; it came into being in 1979. The Court has had a difficult time gaining momentum because relatively few governments have acceded to its jurisdiction (some ten at this writing). The United States has neither ratified the Convention nor accepted the jurisdiction of the Court.

In spite of the tacit security agreement between the OAS partners, U.S. unilateral interventions continued, notably in 1954 in Guatemala, where a democratically elected leftist government was overthrown by a U.S.-backed military force, and in the Dominican Republic, where in 1965 the United States intervened with military force to prevent leftist groups rebelling against a military regime from coming to power. As the cold war made its influence felt, sharply divergent views crystallized between the United States and Latin American nations regarding what constituted security threats. The U.S. propensity for both covert and overt interference to meet what it believed to be security and ideological threats to the region led to a progressive estrangement in U.S.-Latin American relations. At a time when nonintervention in a country's internal affairs was accorded the status of a near-sacred principle in the region, these actions could only resurrect suspicions of a U.S. quest for hegemony. This alienation, together with the stagnation and eventual demise of the Alliance for Progress during the Nixon administration, caused the system to begin to unwind.

In the 1970s, the United States itself turned away from multilateral channels, exhibiting decreased interest in the OAS and shifting its emphasis instead to conventional bilateral diplomatic channels as the chief means of dealing with issues and advancing its interests. In the 1980s, the United States adopted an essentially unilateralist foreign policy, both globally and regionally. Its Central American policy, its position on the Falklands crisis, and its invasion of Grenada all created disillusionment and a sense of aimlessness within the OAS. The 1989 invasion of Panama seemed to be the final nail in the coffin. As one Latin American representative privately observed to the author, the basic question facing the OAS in the 1980s was whether it would survive at all.

Whether in reaction to the thrust of U.S. policy, or to the growing awareness of mutual interdependence, or both, the Latin American countries began moving toward greater coordination among themselves during the 1980s. The Rio Group and the Central American Esquipulas Group are two major examples. The Rio Group formed in January 1983 when the foreign ministers of Mexico, Colombia, Venezuela, and Panama met on Contadora Island, Panama, to organize a mediation of the conflicts in Central America. Two years later, this Contadora Group was joined by a "support group" of Argentina, Brazil, Uruguay, and Peru. The mediation initiative soon stalled, however, and in 1986, when the Central American presidents decided to take things into their own hands and negotiate a peace settlement among themselves, the Contadora and support group decided to transform itself into a permanent mechanism for consultation and policy coordination rather than disband. All South American nations have since been admitted to what is now known as the Rio Group. (Panama, suspended during the Noriega crisis, has not yet been reincorporated.) The Rio Group has also accepted observers from Central America and the Caribbean on a rotating basis. The heads of government of member countries have held annual summit meetings since 1987, their foreign ministers meet frequently, and the Group caucuses in the UN, the OAS, and other international bodies.

The Esquipulas Group (so named for the site in Guatemala at which a final agreement was reached) had its origins in the effort by the Central American presidents to negotiate a homegrown settlement of the Nicaraguan conflict, a task they achieved in 1989 based on the proposals of President Oscar Arias Sánchez of Costa Rica. It too has now become a permanent consultative mechanism with annual summit meetings. The English-speaking Caribbean states have also formed a group, the Organization of Eastern Caribbean States (OECS), which also holds regular summit meetings.

A stirring of renewed cooperation and institutional activity was thus under way by the end of the 1980s, when two watershed events dramatically changed the atmosphere. One was the effective OAS monitoring of the 1990 Nicaraguan general election[8] and the extended monitoring of the *contra* rebel resettlement, which is still taking place more than three years later, as part of the peace settlement that made the elections possible. This broke new ground in the collective defense of democracy, and it has been followed by successful monitoring of a series of other elections in the hemisphere. The second was the proposal by the United States for the Enterprise for the Americas Initiative (EAI). That proposal, put forth by President Bush in a speech on June 27, 1990, contained three parts: steps to forgive part of the debt owed to official U.S. agencies, steps to increase private foreign investment in the region, and a proposed free trade area "from Alaska to Patagonia." The EAI elicited a strong positive response in Latin America, where it was perceived as an invitation to negotiate and solve problems jointly, rather than through the traditional blueprint presented by the United States on a take-it-or-leave-it basis. The breadth and scope of the vision—the concept of a free trade area for the whole hemisphere—carried a momentum of its own.

The sense that the world was at a historic moment, with new challenges and opportunities, was explicitly recognized by the OAS member states at their 21st General Assembly held in Santiago in June 1991. In a landmark document approved by the assembly on June 4, 1991, "The Santiago Commitment to Democracy and the Renewal of the Inter

American System" (the full text is in Appendix 1), the American governments, noting that the depolarization and lessening of world tensions had paved the way for "concerted action by all countries through global and regional organizations," declared "their firm resolve to stimulate the renewal of the Organization of American States, to make it more effective and useful in the application of its guiding principles and for the attainment of its objectives."

The Santiago Commitment represented, in effect, a comprehensive restatement of the organization's basic goals and purposes. Its approval, along with the promulgation of other significant documents, made the 21st General Assembly a milestone in the organization's history. Indeed, it would not overstate the case by much to suggest a comparison with the Ninth Inter-American Conference of American States in Bogotá in 1948, which promulgated the OAS Charter itself. Both responded to the opening for new relationships and cooperation among the region's states created by the end of major global conflicts.

In Latin America, two mutually reinforcing currents that emerged in the 1980s—a growing agreement on what makes for sound macroeconomic policy, and an even stronger consensus on constitutional democracy as the desirable political model—provided greater common ground and a more collegial atmosphere than had been possible in earlier times when conflicting ideological and structural models competed for allegiance in the region. Combined with the impact of the revolutionary events taking place across the globe, this led to a change in Latin America's approach to the United States. Whereas, in the past, Latin American countries tended to define their policies and strategies as efforts to counterbalance U.S. power, they have increasingly come to see the support and cooperation of the United States as important to the successful management of the major problems confronting them.

Viewed from the other side, the cooperation of Latin America and the Caribbean has become increasingly important and relevant to the United States. Today the destiny of the United States appears more bound up with that of the hemisphere than ever before across a whole range of issues that directly affects the well-being of its economy and society—trade, energy, immigration, investments, environment, drugs. If European and Asian blocs develop that are competitive vis-a-vis the rest of the world rather than cooperative, the hemisphere will look better and better as a partner.

This growth in the mutuality of interest and purpose is not necessarily, of course, a permanent or irreversible condition. It is entirely possible that the next few years could see rising inter-American conflict—over trade policy, economic strategies, ethnic rivalries, competition for power and influence, migration flows, and the external consequences of domestic political turbulence—particularly if major actors (like the United States) are insensitive to or misread the region's dynamics; frictions could grow if such a state turned to protectionist, nationalist, punitive, or interventionist strategies. Moreover, twelve countries in Latin America and the Caribbean will have held general elections for new governments by the end of 1994.[9] Speculation and concern about what the results may be, as well as the uncertainty felt in Latin America and the Caribbean regarding the future course of the Clinton administration's hemispheric and global foreign policy, have contributed to a growing sense of caution and apprehension in the region. In this climate, the negotiations over the North American Free Trade Agreement (NAFTA) among the United States, Canada, and Mexico have come to epitomize the hopes and anxieties of all the countries in the area. A failure to conclude NAFTA—or even a prolonged, indefinite delay—would have a markedly chilling impact on U.S.-Latin American relations and on the foundation of shared values and ideas that currently underpins them.

CHAPTER 3

THE SUBSTANTIVE AGENDA

The current agenda and concerns of the OAS are nowhere more succinctly summarized than in the "Santiago Commitment": promoting and defending democracy and human rights, stimulating economic and social development, combating poverty, supporting economic integration, fostering educational, scientific, and cultural exchanges, fighting drug trafficking, protecting the environment, and redefining hemispheric security.[1] Space limitations preclude comprehensive treatment of OAS activity, but this section will briefly survey the major areas of concern with special focus on the promotion and defense of democracy.

THE ECONOMIC SECTOR

The OAS has not played a major operating role in the economic area since the demise of the Alliance for Progress and the annual country reviews. Over the past two decades, it has been consumed with its role as a provider of technical assistance, and in terms of broader economic questions, it has served essentially only as a forum for discussion.

Although the hemispheric agenda today is dominated by trade, investment, and development, the OAS does not have the technical reach or the organizational design to be the central operating institution in economic affairs. Most of the hemisphere's international economic relations are carried out through bilateral government channels or a mix of regional and global institutions, like the Inter-American Development Bank, the World Bank, the International Monetary Fund, GATT, and the region's own economic subsystems. That will surely continue to be the case.

Up to the present, the OAS has operated in the economic sector through two separate councils: the Inter-American Council on Education, Science and Culture (CIECC) and the Inter-American Economic and Social Council (CIES), each with a permanent executive committee and program and budget subcommittee. (Appendix 4 describes the organizational structure of the OAS and its various policymaking bodies.) In a special session at the 23d General Assembly, held in Managua in June 1993, the member states approved an amendment to the OAS Charter (the "Protocol of Managua") that combines CIES and CIECC into a single council, the Inter-American Council for Integral Development (CIDI).[?] Since a Charter amendment creates CIDI, that amendment will not come into effect until ratified by two-thirds of the member states. Essentially, the purpose of this amendment is to streamline and consolidate the management of the technical assistance programs now under CIES and CIECC, and to combine their secretariat support, thereby reducing overhead costs and eliminating duplication. The OAS has engaged in technical assistance activities since 1952 in such areas as basic and vocational education, regional and river basin development, small business development, science and engineering development, and similar fields. Though small in size and probably overly fragmented across a number of discrete areas, these offerings occupy a unique niche. Other agencies, such as the World Bank and the Inter-American Development Bank, support larger programs, but only in connection with their own loan projects and priorities. The OAS meets direct requests from its members and concentrates on human resource development.

The very small countries, especially the Caribbean nations, consider these programs essential because they have little access to alternative sources for technical advice and training. They have expressed strong concern that emphasis on peacekeeping or support for democracy not be at the expense of technical assistance programs.

The broad language of the Charter amendment on CIDI ("to promote cooperation among the American States [to achieve] integral development and . . . eliminate extreme poverty in accordance with the standards of the Charter") suggests that the council could broaden its activity beyond technical assistance if it so chose. The amendment gives it the power to establish nonpermanent subcommittees and subsidiary bodies, and it specifies that CIDI must meet at the ministerial level at least once a year. The council may also call meetings at the ministerial level for the "specialized or sectorial topics" it considers relevant.

Until CIDI comes into being with the amendment's ratification, CIES and CIECC continue to exist and function. CIECC has been the focal point for national ministers of education and culture to meet and interact. These officials found the CIECC useful as a way to develop and coordinate their nations' educational and cultural policies and programs. (The provisions giving CIDI power to convene ministerial-level meetings reflect that experience.)

CIES, once the focal point of serious policy deliberations, especially in the 1950s and 1960s, has not fared as well; it was never able to involve the economic staffs of member governments on a regular basis as CIECC did with its relevant ministries. CIES and its supporting staff in the OAS Secretariat have concentrated on technical assistance programs, while new hemispheric economic initiatives, such as EAI and environmental protection, have been entrusted to specially created committees of the OAS Permanent Council. The Special Committee for Consultation and Negotiation (CECON), established under CIES in 1969 to address issues involving significant economic policy questions, degenerated over time into an arena for confrontation and deadlock and gradually fell into ineffectiveness and disuse.[3]

Another major and more immediately important change made by the Managua General Assembly was the conversion of CECON into a Special Committee for Trade (CEC).[4] CEC is to focus on trade matters and issues. Its role, as described in the establishing resolution, is to monitor the trade liberalization and expansion process; to disseminate information and analysis thereon; to promote the exchange of views on trade issues; to study trade conditions and "offer suggestions" for improving them among the member states; and to "encourage the measures required to reach this objective." The negotiation role, which proved such a stumbling block in the case of CECON, has been dropped.

The structural characteristics of CEC also reflect lessons learned from CECON's experience: member states are to be represented on the committee by "senior officials in the area of trade policy," and CEC meetings may be held at "the Commerce Minister level," again following the CIECC pattern. In addition, an advisory group of nine "senior governmental officials from the trade area" is to be established, as well as a high-level technical unit to analyze and collect information. Decisions are to be adopted by consensus. Because CEC was established under the general powers given to the General Assembly to create special committees or commissions, it does not require ratification; it comes into being immediately.

The focus on monitoring, exchange of information and analysis, and policy dialogue should make CEC very helpful to member states and to the process of trade integration at both the subregional and regional levels since the dynamic trade sector currently has no active hemispheric forum of this kind. If the trade and economic integration envisioned in the EAI flourish, some additional multilateral architecture may be needed. In most cases, though, the trade agreements themselves will provide the structure for dispute settlement. Other needs will almost surely be met by ad hoc arrangements that the OAS could facilitate through CEC.

The changes adopted with respect to CEC and CIDI are the culmination of some two years of internal consultation and discussion, and they reflect the members' consensus that OAS economic activities require reorganization to make them more relevant to the circumstances and needs of the 1990s. The changes are significant in this sense because they put the OAS in a position to play a genuine policy role in discussion of economic issues and their relationship to other goals, exchange of information, and suggestion of recommendations to the member governments and to relevant international economic institutions like the Inter-American Development Bank or the United Nations Economic Commission for Latin America and the Caribbean. This kind of norm-generating, monitoring role was precisely the one recommended by a recent Blue Ribbon Consultative Group formed to evaluate the OAS,[5] and appears to be the direction in which the member states may seek to move the organization.

As the emphasis on promoting democracy has grown, Latin American states have also become increasingly concerned with the connection of economic and social development to the maintenance of democratic systems, and they have sought in various ways to emphasize this linkage in OAS activities. The Sixteenth Special Session of the General Assembly, held in Washington in December 1992, approved amendments to the OAS Charter with regard to defense of democracy (the "Protocol of Washington"). It also approved amendments stressing the need to "eradicate extreme poverty," calling its elimination "an essential part of the promotion and the consolidation of representative democracy."[6] At Managua, the member states approved the convocation of a Special Session of the General Assembly on Inter-American Cooperation for Development, to be held in Mexico during the first quarter of 1994, "to orchestrate schemes and mechanisms of cooperation for comprehensive development, the struggle against extreme poverty, and improvement of basic levels of social and economic well-being in the hemisphere."[7]

THE POLITICAL SECTOR

Political affairs, and dispute settlement and conflict management in particular, are at the center of the OAS mandate under its Charter, and the organization has a long and respectable history in these areas. Moreover, the OAS is the only regionwide organization available to the member states for these purposes.

These political functions are now more relevant than ever for two reasons. First, territorial disputes are still one of the potential causes of interstate conflict in the hemisphere, and some of these continue to simmer beneath the surface. In the past twenty-five years, blood has been shed in the cases of the El Salvador/Honduras, Ecuador/Peru, and Falkland/Malvinas disputes. The last two remain essentially unresolved, as do border claims between Colombia and Venezuela and Venezuela and Guyana, as well as the question of Bolivian access to the sea.

Second, whereas most of the OAS conflict resolution efforts in the past dealt with disputes between states, the recent threats to the peace have increasingly come from internal situations—insurgencies and civil wars—which the OAS once largely finessed because of the domestic jurisdiction question. There are currently three internal conflicts—in Guatemala, Colombia, and Peru—in which major human rights violations have occurred. Each of these has the potential to explode into serious threats to the region's peace. The Santiago Commitment to defend democracy, which by definition involves domestic matters, now makes internal conflict a problem directly relevant to the OAS agenda.

OAS activity in the field of human rights is based upon the 1948 American Declaration of the Rights and Duties of Man and the 1969 American Convention on Human Rights, referred to above. The Inter-American Commission on Human Rights (IACHR) and the still-developing Inter-American Court on Human Rights give the OAS an active, and frequently forceful, role in this field. Through both persuasion and published reports, the IACHR has been instrumental in improving member government observance of basic rights. It prepares an annual report, with sections on countries and individual cases, as well as special reports. Over its life, it has effectively challenged abuses by authoritarian regimes; made contributions to transitional processes toward democracy, perhaps most dramatically in Argentina, Nicaragua, and El Salvador; and contributed to a broader awakening of civil society throughout the region. The multilateral judgment represented by the commission's reports carries considerable weight in conferring or denying legitimacy to governments in the practice of civil liberties.

Although nominated by governments, the seven members of the IACHR are elected in their own right and not as representatives of their countries.[8] The IACHR's autonomy is further enhanced by its prerogative to initiate investigations without the approval of either the secretary-general or the Permanent Council. Its structure thus gives it a useful dual character as an organ of an intergovernmental body, capable of acting in the name of that body, and, at the same time, possessing operational independence.

The work of the IACHR is, however, becoming both more complicated and more sensitive. Dealing with abuses by dictatorial governments is one thing, but dealing with human rights considerations in democratic regimes is something else. With democratic values comes the promise of justice and the rule of law. Hence an increase is to be expected in the number of grievants taking that prospect at face value. The absence of dictatorships also makes human rights abuses from other quarters, such as terrorists, more apparent. And the urge to fight "fire with fire" can sorely tempt constitutional authority to commit abuses.

Some elected governments in the region have, in fact, become very sensitive to IACHR criticism. Some have suggested that the scope of the commission's activity be curbed—for example, eliminating investigations and reports on individual cases of torture and disappearance in favor of broader studies on generic problems like the rights of the handicapped, or restricting its authority to condemn abuse or to comment on the adequacy or fairness of electoral systems, limiting its writ to giving advice to governments. Such sentiments are in the minority, but they demonstrate how touchy some governments still are about "intervention" in their domestic affairs.

Narcotics is another political policy area of specific concern. The OAS functions in this field through the Inter-American Drug Abuse Control Commission (CICAD).[9] CICAD focuses on nonenforcement aspects of the fight against drugs, specifically strengthening national and international narcotics legislation; stimulating prevention measures and public awareness; and sponsoring and disseminating information, advice, and research results through seminars, conferences, and other means of forging links among national agencies, international institutions, and nongovernmental organizations engaged in the fight against drugs. CICAD's achievements have been impressive. A notable example was the preparation of model regulations regarding control of chemical precursors and money laundering. Although suggestions have been made from time to time that the OAS develop an enforcement capacity—an OAS drug force—these have engendered no real support but some active opposition among member governments.

THE SECURITY SECTOR

Collective security[10] was one of the original objectives of the OAS. Both the OAS Charter and the Inter-American Treaty of Reciprocal Assistance (the Rio Pact) became basic parts of the formal institutional machinery of the cold war. The Rio Pact, signed in 1947, a year before the Charter, is a classic collective-security treaty and permits the levying of sanctions, including the use of force, in cases of aggression and armed attack. It has not been used in recent years. Last invoked by Argentina in the Malvinas (Falkland Islands) dispute with Britain in 1982, it proved ineffective. Although technically still in force, the general consensus is that it is no longer functionally useful.

Although cold war security concerns are now obsolete, how to define collective security in the hemisphere today is still a matter of spirited debate. Cross-border attacks are not what states fear most today; rather their concern is with conflict having internal societal origins. A number of social phenomena—poverty, corruption, terrorism, human rights, drugs, migration—have taken precedence over secure boundaries at the heart of the concept of security.

In Santiago, in June 1991, the member states agreed in a Canadian-sponsored resolution that the themes of defense expenditures, acquisition and proliferation of weapons systems, and confidence-building measures were legitimate security concerns confronting the region.[11] The Santiago assembly established a security working group to make recommendations in these areas. A year later, in Nassau, the member states approved an extensive statement of principles and goals entitled "Cooperation for Security and Development in the Hemisphere—Regional Contributions to Global Security," representing in effect a normative framework to guide member governments' activities in these areas.[12] The document not only stresses the relevance of socioeconomic conditions to security but urges specific goals and objectives with regard to controlling armaments, improving transparency in arms acquisition and arms control processes, and supporting UN and global efforts in these areas. The assembly also converted the security working group into a special committee, the Special Committee on Hemispheric Security, to continue to work on a security agenda.

The Managua General Assembly renewed the Special Committee's mandate and asked it to give priority consideration to the following matters: the OAS-UN relationship in matters of regional security; global and regional disarmament and arms control; the relationship of arms limitations to development and environmental matters; prevention of proliferation of weapons of mass destruction; transparency in arms acquisitions and transfers; improving conflict prevention and dispute settlement measures; confidence-building steps and military/technical information exchange; and civil-military relations.[13]

The security agenda that the organization is developing covers current themes that have relevance on the global scene as well. All the resolutions referred to above call for close consultation with the United Nations and related organizations, such as the International Atomic Energy Agency, and for keeping them fully informed. The civil-military topic is particularly worth noting in this regard. Translating the various resolutions' norms and goals into practical measures will not be easy. Indeed, the long period of time the special committee has taken to develop recommendations is the consequence of the careful discussion and consensus-building process through which the OAS typically proceeds.

The Nassau General Assembly held in May 1992 had also asked the Permanent Council to make recommendations defining the "legal-institutional relationship" between the Inter-American Defense Board (IADB) and the OAS. The status of the IADB is a sensitive matter because it brings into play basic questions regarding civil-military relations and democracy. The concern is twofold: in the post-cold war world the IADB has an uncertain purpose and agenda; and it has up to now constituted, in effect, a separate organization of hemisphere military forces, which have tended to see it as their organization, independent of the "political" organs of the OAS.[14]

At the 23d General Assembly in Managua, the member governments ducked the issue for now, calling for continued study and for a report to be made to the next general assembly in 1994. This reflected the need felt for further "ripening" of the consensus-building process. However, the Assembly did provide that, until final redefinition is determined, all the political organs (the Permanent Council, the Meetings of Foreign Ministers, and the General Assemblies) may call on the Defense Board for "technical-military advisory services and consultancy." [15]

The redefinition of the Defense Board's mission and status remains controversial and various proposals have been put forward. Some members favor converting the Defense Board into an advisory and supporting entity for the Permanent Council under its general supervision. Others propose converting it into a specialized organization, like the Pan-American Health Organization. Some would prefer making no changes, fearing that any redefinition would provide the OAS (and the United States) with an additional tool (and temptation) to interfere in members' internal affairs. A few would just as soon eliminate the Defense Board altogether, but realize that this suggestion is unlikely to prosper.

PROMOTION AND DEFENSE OF DEMOCRACY

The proclamation of democracy as a basic value of the American states goes back a long way in the documentary history of the hemisphere, though such a noble declaration has been honored in the breach more often than not. It has evolved, as one Latin American scholar and diplomat put it, "from a moral commitment to a juridical obligation enshrined in the Charter."[16] The OAS Charter declares that its goals "require" representative democracy.[17]

The geopolitics of the cold war plus the rise in the number of dictatorships in the region in the 1950s and 1960s weakened and complicated the various members' commitment to democratic government.[18] During the 1970s, however, public support for human rights and international criticism of authoritarian abuses increased. With the spread of democratic government throughout the hemisphere in the 1980s, the commitment to the principle of representative democracy was restored.

Reforms to the Charter, approved in 1985 by a special session of the General Assembly meeting in Cartagena, Colombia (the Protocol of Cartagena), inserted new language in the Charter's preamble reasserting the essentiality of the democratic political model.[19] In the Santiago Commitment, the member states declared "their inescapable commitment" to democracy. The 22d General Assembly meeting in Nassau reaffirmed these points in the "Declaration of Nassau."

An even more historic and substantive achievement was the approval by the 21st General Assembly in Santiago of Resolution 1080 (text is in Appendix 2), which created an automatic procedure for convening the hemisphere's foreign ministers in the event of a coup or other interruption of legitimately elected government "to look into the events collectively and adopt any decisions deemed appropriate." This resolution provided the legal basis for OAS action with regard to Haiti, Peru, and Guatemala, as will be discussed further on.

The 16th Special Session of the General Assembly, convened in Washington in December 1992, agreed to amend the OAS Charter by inserting a new article (new Article 9) giving the General Assembly the power to suspend from membership by a two-thirds vote a government that overthrows a democratic regime (the "Protocol of Washington").[20] The protocol was approved by a vote of 31-1-1, with Mexico voting against and Trinidad and Tobago abstaining. Although Mexico lobbied other members very hard, it was in the end isolated in its opposition to the measure. The protocol is now pending ratification by the member states.

Resolution 1080 and the Article 9 reform are OAS landmarks. For the first time in the organization's history, a particular domestic political circumstance—the interruption of democratic government—is declared to be grounds for collective action.

The "Declaration of Managua," approved by the 23d General Assembly in June 1993, is yet another noteworthy document on democracy. It elaborates on the meaning of the commitment to democracy in terms of the goals members are obligated to seek. For example, members are to strive to modernize domestic administrative and political structures and systems, improve public administration, protect minorities and political opposition groups, achieve national reconciliation and consolidate a "democratic culture," meet basic human needs, safeguard human rights, and ensure the subordination of armed forces to legitimately constituted civilian authority. The protocol also declared that the OAS mission is not limited simply to defending democracy when it is attacked but must also include efforts "to prevent and anticipate the very causes of the problems that work against democratic rule." (The text of the Declaration is in Appendix 3.)

The OAS has gradually stretched the limits of collective jurisdiction not only in passing resolutions but in its operational precedents as well. In 1979, for example, the 17th Meeting of Consultation of Foreign Ministers called for the replacement of a sitting government (the Somoza regime in Nicaragua) and laid down specific criteria for that purpose; this kind of affront to sovereignty would have been unheard of a few years earlier.[21]

In 1990, the OAS took proactive steps to implement the commitment to democracy. Responding to a resolution approved by the 20th General Assembly, the secretary-general established in the Secretariat a "Unit for Democratic Development" intended to provide advisory services (research, training, information exchange) and direct assistance (election monitoring, technical assistance, and other aid requested by member states).[22] The unit's staff has established three priorities for its agenda: technical support to electoral organizations, legislative training, and civic education. Dissatisfaction with this agenda as being too timid and too limited has been growing among the OAS ambassadors. In addition, the secretary-general has organized a process of civilian election-monitoring missions. Since 1989, fifteen such missions have been carried out, eight of them covering an extended period from voter and candidate registration to the ballot counts and official proclamation of returns. OAS election monitoring has become for the international community a widely respected assessment of the legitimacy of an election, something that is carried over to the government chosen.

The OAS mission to oversee and facilitate the peace settlement in Nicaragua set a new precedent, but it is curious how unaware the general public—in the United States at least—has been of its key contribution. Although the 1990 Nicaraguan elections were also monitored by missions from the UN and the European Community, as well as a large number of private groups, the OAS mission, with more than four hundred members, was the largest. Moreover, it began its operations some seven months prior to the election in order to monitor the campaign period, and it provided the communications and transportation infrastructure that aided other missions observing the election to function during the voting period.

The OAS-supervised International Commission for Support and Verification (CIAV/OAS), assigned to monitor and facilitate the resettlement of *contra* rebels, has been working in Nicaragua for three years now. In response to a Nicaraguan government request that the OAS develop a broad-based support program, the organization decided in June 1993 to extend the CIAV/OAS presence and activities for two more years; in addition, it approved OAS assistance to the government in strengthening legal, policing, and electoral institutions, and in civic education for internal reconciliation.[23] Nicaragua may again become a major OAS concern, however, in view of the recent political deterioration and increase in violence in that country.

Suriname requested OAS oversight of a peace agreement concluded in August 1992 between the government and two insurgent forces. With the agreement of both sides, the secretary-general established a mission that monitored and facilitated the implementation of the agreement, including the disarming of the insurgent groups and the destruction of their weapons.[24]

All the activities described up to now were based on the consent of the governments and forces involved. A very different challenge was presented by the interruptions of democratic rule in Haiti, Peru, and Guatemala, which directly posed the enforcement question: What should be done to restore democratic rule when it has been broken?

In the Peruvian case, President Alberto Fujimori, in an action backed by the military and apparently with substantial public support, shut down the Congress and the judicial system on April 5, 1992, and began ruling by decree. Fujimori responded to demands of the OAS that democratic processes be restored, as well as to general international condemnation, by formally committing himself, at the Nassau General Assembly, to a gradual restoration of democratic procedures: elections for a new Congress and a constituent assembly (held November 22, 1992); acceptance of OAS monitoring of that election; and agreement to an investigation of the human rights situation by the IACHR.

The prompt condemnation of his actions by the OAS and the diplomatic isolation it portended, as well as accompanying voluntary steps by international donors (especially the Inter-American Development Bank) in temporarily suspending loan disbursements, touched a nerve with Fujimori. One of Peru's major objectives had been the restoration of its credibility and status in the international financial community. The desire to avoid becoming a regional pariah was clearly a consideration in Fujimori's decision to retreat at least partway from his earlier action, and to appear personally before the OAS General Assembly to do so. On December 14, 1992, the OAS accepted Fujimori's commitments, asked that the Peruvian government keep it informed of its evolution back to democracy, and closed its consideration of the Peruvian case.[25] It remains to be seen, of course, how genuine the movement back to constitutional democracy will turn out to be.

By contrast, the May 25, 1993, attempt by Guatemalan president Jorge Serrano Elias to seize power by dissolving Congress and suspending the Constitution in a similar "auto-coup" collapsed within days. Although the military high command initially supported Serrano, it withdrew its support in the face of remarkably unified and, for Guatemala, vehement opposition from all sectors of the nation's civil society, as well as equally unanimous condemnation by the international community. Serrano was forced to resign, and left the country. An effort by the military high command to install Serrano's vice president as chief executive also collapsed in the face of determined opposition from business, political, and church circles, and even from within the junior officer ranks of the military itself. The crisis was resolved within ten days, when all parties acquiesced in the congressional election, according to constitutional procedures, of an interim president to complete Serrano's term. The remarkable choice was Ramiro de Leon Carpio, the country's foremost human rights ombudsman, who immediately and successfully replaced the minister of defense and the army high command.

That the crisis turned out as it did was due in large measure to the sweeping, forceful, and simultaneous reaction of Guatemala's domestic society and the international community. Had only one group reacted, the military high command might have ridden out the storm. Also critical was pressure from two countries with important ties to Guatemala, Mexico and the United States. The suspension of development aid by international donors weighed heavily, especially the U.S. threat to cancel the tariff concessions that Guatemala enjoyed, which would have seriously damaged the large and important nontraditional export industry that had grown up in the country. The business community was thus strongly motivated to demand a return to constitutional order.

An OAS fact-finding team under the secretary-general, which had been authorized almost immediately by the Permanent Council, arrived in Guatemala at a crucial moment in the internal maneuvering. Most observers present in Guatemala at the time agree that the team's

presence and its discussions with all parties were helpful in crystalliz-
ing the momentum for restoration of democratic procedures. On June
8, the Meeting of Foreign Ministers that had been convened to take up
the Guatemala case declared the crisis solved and closed its session.[26]
The task of consolidating democracy in Guatemala still lies ahead of the
new president, of course. But the crisis revealed that the country's civil
society was far stronger and the rejection of a return to military rule far
deeper than anyone had realized, including the Guatemalans themselves. That gives grounds for hope.

The Haitian case—chronologically the first to test the Santiago
Commitment—has been far more difficult to handle. On September 30,
1991, the Haitian army ousted President Jean-Bertrand Aristide, the
country's first-ever freely elected president, nine months after he had
taken office. The immediate international reaction outside the hemisphere was passive; the UN Security Council, for example, found itself
unable to meet on the problem (for reasons that will be explained later).
It was the quick condemnation of the coup by the OAS, acting under
Resolution 1080, and its recommendations for diplomatic and economic sanctions that shaped the subsequent international response. The
principle that the resolution of the crisis had to be based on Aristide's
restoration to office (that is, the coup's reversal), which became the central goal of all subsequent international mediation efforts, was first set
out by the OAS. There is little doubt that only the prompt OAS response
prevented the Haitian military from legitimating their coup and making
it permanent.

Despite the sanctions, yearlong efforts by the OAS to mediate an
agreement between Aristide and the Haitian military stalled owing to
the intransigence of both sides. Increasingly concerned over the domestic political consequences of a massive Haitian refugee flow, the United
States in November 1992 sought the involvement of the United Nations.
In early December, UN secretary-general Boutros Boutros-Ghali and
OAS secretary-general Joao Baena Soares agreed to appoint jointly former Argentine foreign minister Dante Caputo as their personal representative, and the Argentine statesman assumed the leadership of a
joint OAS/UN mediation effort.

Although Caputo did, in early 1993, secure the agreement of all
parties to the dispatch of a relatively large mission of civilian human
rights observers to Haiti (the International Civilian Mission to Haiti
OAS/UN),[27] his effort to mediate a political agreement stalled. In June
1993, Haiti was placed on the UN Security Council agenda through the
efforts of the United States, Canada, Venezuela, and France (the so-called
Friends of Haiti).[28] On June 25, 1993, the Council, acting under Chapter

VII of the UN Charter, imposed a worldwide mandatory oil and weapons embargo on Haiti, as well as a freeze of Haiti's assets abroad.[29] (The nonbinding OAS sanctions had been ignored by non-Western Hemisphere countries, and even by some Latin American countries.) It is important to observe that since defense of democracy is no ground for UN action, the Security Council justified its decision on the argument that the Haitian situation was a threat to international peace.

The pressure created by the binding nature of the UN embargo enabled the OAS/UN mediator to conclude an agreement on July 3, 1993, between Aristide and the Haitian military. It is a complicated agreement, dependent on a careful sequence of events—including designation of a new prime minister, retirement of Commander in Chief Raoul Cedras and reformation of the army general staff, and creation of a new police force—all culminating in Aristide's return by October 30, 1993. The pact is fragile, and the distrust and suspicion between the parties is deep and visceral. It is unclear whether it will succeed. The task now facing the OAS and the UN is twofold: insuring observance of the agreement's terms and mounting an external aid effort to restore the economy and build a democratic structure. A large OAS and UN presence will almost surely be needed to accomplish both objectives, and planning has been in process for both purposes for some time, including the organization of an international police mission under UN authority to maintain order.

Some tentative initial conclusions can be drawn from the experience in these three cases. First, Resolution 1080 works. In each case, the organization's prompt response was important in stimulating and shaping the general international reaction and preventing the democratic breakdown from being legitimated. Second, international pressure works. Fear of being isolated diplomatically and appearing as pariahs was clearly a deterrent in the Peruvian and Guatemalan cases. On the other hand, the threat of international disapproval had little effect on the Haitian military, given the relatively primitive civic structure and the fact that Haiti was already on the margins of international concern and awareness.

Economic pressures can also contribute to a solution if they are strategically targeted on those segments of the population that need to be influenced. This was the case in both Peru and Guatemala. The OAS sanctions on Haiti were too indiscriminate and leaky to have any impact on the supporters of the military coup, whereas the targeted and compulsory nature of the UN oil embargo and freezing of external assets did have an effect.

It is also evident that the attitudes of and pressures exerted by individual countries with special ties to the problem are extremely important.

The United States was in this sense central to all three cases. A number of observers and analysts believe, in fact, that the Haitian case dragged on for so long because for the first eighteen months Washington's diplomacy conveyed mixed signals, leading many to conclude that the United States was not sure it wanted to see Aristide restored to power. Whether or not that was the case, the Clinton administration, under domestic pressure on the Haitian refugee problem, took special pains after it gained office to send a clear, unambiguous message that the United States wanted Aristide and democratic rule restored as soon as possible and would use whatever pressure necessary to achieve that objective.

The interesting point is that the efficacy of pressure and actions by nations individually can be amplified by being channeled, focused, and coordinated through the OAS or the UN. In the Haitian case, the United States clearly placed its support behind the OAS/UN mediation rather than autonomously exert its own power. The OAS/UN mediator was the one visible actor, directing a multilateral effort. Perhaps, as one commentator speculated, "with crises sprouting around the world Washington was anxious to develop effective joint strategies for dealing with them."[30]

In addition to these three cases, the hemisphere's commitment to democratic rule was strengthened when two of the region's major countries, Brazil and Venezuela, used constitutional procedures to resolve peacefully serious domestic political crises that a decade ago would almost surely have provoked a military coup. In each country, charges of corruption and overwhelming popular demands for the removal of the president (Fernando Collor de Mello in Brazil and Carlos Andres Pérez in Venezuela) led to the impeachment of the chief executive and the selection of an interim successor according to constitutional procedures—and to the preservation of democratic rule. The Venezuelan case was all the more gratifying because the building crisis had already led to two failed military coup attempts, in February and November 1992.

The OAS commitment to democracy obviously entails proactive as well as reactive dimensions. Historically, the OAS has only reacted after a conflict explodes into a crisis. The conviction is growing, however, that the organization must now become proactive in helping member governments consolidate democratic systems and in preventing crises from developing. The need to confront the underlying causes of democratic breakdown—poverty, underdevelopment, social injustices, inadequate political and judicial institutions—is widely accepted among the member states. That, indeed, was the basic thrust of the Declaration of Managua, which many OAS representatives see as a warrant for

developing new activities and incentives to help member states meet
problems before they get out of hand.

Establishing a particular political concept—democracy—as a principle to which member states are committed is an unusual step for an
international organization. It has been possible in the case of the OAS
because of the regional nature of the organization, that is, because of the
relative homogeneousness of the member states, their experiences, and
their traditions.[31] It has not been possible on a global scale. The meaning
and limitations of this point, in terms of both traditional international
law and practical politics, were provocatively summarized by
Ambassador Bernardo Pericas Neto, the Brazilian representative to the
OAS, in his capacity as chairman of the preparatory working group for
the Washington Protocol meeting:

> The effective exercise of representative democracy as a
> basis for the solidarity of the member states is included
> among the principles of the Charter of the OAS. It is
> not, however, a principle of international law. It cannot
> be invoked or defended as a principle in any context
> other than that of the present Charter of the OAS. . . .
> The requirement of the effective exercise of represen-
> tative democracy is a principle applied to the member
> states of the OAS purely as members of the regional
> organization, and only concerns relations that are
> developed in the specific context of this organization. It
> clearly does not apply to the bilateral relations of the
> member states of the OAS—only to the extent that each
> one unilaterally and in its sovereign capacity so wish-
> es. It would in fact be incongruous to seek to force the
> states of the Americas to mete out to one another a
> more restrictive treatment than that which they grant to
> the States of other regions of the world.[32]

The question of promoting and defending democracy, in short, runs
squarely into the fundamental tension between the proposition that the
OAS ought to ensure in practice what it defines as principle and the
abiding allegiance to the talisman of "sovereignty." The task of supporting democracy thus encounters virtually all the conceptual hurdles, conflicts, and dilemmas that affect OAS prospects across the whole
spectrum of its activity.

CHAPTER 4

OBSTACLES AND DILEMMAS CONFRONTING THE OAS

STRUCTURAL UNDERPINNINGS

The nature of the OAS is defined and delimited by its structure. Its legal framework, its subsidiary policymaking infrastructure, its financial setup, its characteristic composition and relations with the member states and with the United Nations, all these architectonics help determine the range and effectiveness of OAS ventures.

POWER ASYMMETRY: THE UNITED STATES AND LATIN AMERICA. The substantial difference in power between the United States and the other nations of the hemisphere has been the greatest impulse for and at the same time the greatest impediment to effective inter-American relations. Much of the modern history of U.S.-Latin American relations can be interpreted in terms of the efforts of the United States to legitimate and exercise its power in the region, and of the Latin Americans to constrain and cope with it.

The relatively sudden catapulting of the United States into superpower status at the end of World War II facilitated the extension of U.S. influence throughout the hemisphere. Many U.S. citizens have reflexively assumed that the dominance the United States exercised through most of the cold war period represents the "normal" state of affairs, and that U.S. leadership is in the natural order of things. The sense of mission inherent in U.S. "exceptionalism," moreover, has always compelled rationalization of U.S. self-interest in terms of appeals to larger ideals: to protect the hemisphere, defend freedom, promote the region's welfare. The United States has traditionally tended to see the institutions of the inter-American system as instruments for marshaling hemispheric support for U.S. policies and objectives, that is, as an alliance under its leadership.

Latin American nations, on the other hand, have always considered the protection of their national autonomy, especially in relation to U.S. power, as a basic foreign policy goal. They have consistently used a strategy of resorting to international forums and to juridical obligations and commitments as the way to secure restraint from the United States. Latin Americans thus traditionally tend to see the treaties and institutions of the system as a way to shackle Gulliver. Over time, however, some governments have come to see the OAS less as a defense than as vulnerable to U.S. dominance. Proposals to improve the effectiveness of the OAS, or expand the scope of its responsibilities, reflexively rekindle historic fears of U.S. dominance. This results in wariness and, for some, a kind of congenital opposition.

The pattern of asymmetry, like many power relationships, was affected by the changes accompanying the Soviet Union's collapse. The United States is no longer the dominating giant it was after World War II, nor does it now have the resources to exercise hegemony. Increased self-confidence and national capabilities on the part of Latin American countries, part of a general diffusion of power throughout the world, have softened the polarization and the hard edges of asymmetry. One of the felicitous consequences of this historical moment is that the convergence of interests of countries in the hemisphere has permitted the passage of the OAS from an arena of bipolar confrontation to one in which a more constructive agenda based on shared views is collegially discussed. Yet historical experiences and differing psychological and perceptual vantage points continue to influence the relationship. Culturally, the U.S. public has never empathized very greatly with Latin America. There has long been among many in this country a kind of subconscious condescending view of the countries to the south. This patronizing attitude, when combined with the "can do" quality of the U.S. character, reinforces the instinct for the unilateral use of power.

The main point of reference for Latin American nationalism and aspirations is still the United States. But suspicions about U.S. motivations are never far below the surface. A Latin American perception of the United States as presumptuous (or in Spanish, *prepotente*) is not all that uncommon. Such feelings, moreover, are resuscitated by episodes such as the 1989 U.S. invasion of Panama or the assertion of the right to enforce U.S. law extraterritorially, as in the case of the Cuban

Democracy Act (previously known as the Torricelli bill) forbidding foreign subsidiaries of U.S. multinationals from trading with Cuba.

HETEROGENOUS MEMBERSHIP. Perhaps the major change wrought in the OAS since its founding was the admission of twelve English-speaking Caribbean states (thirteen if Suriname, which often associates with the group, is included), according them the same status as all other members. Differences in size, population, and power between these and the other members is marked, and, language aside, there are differences in political culture and tradition. Tactically, these thirteen states frequently function as a bloc. Hence, the larger Latin American countries now confront an asymmetry problem of their own; they are uncomfortable with the prospect that these thirteen states can determine to a considerable degree what the organization does or does not do, even though in their totality they hardly approximate the political or economic weight of even a single average-sized Latin American country.

Another important change was Canada's full accession to membership. Canada's presence diffuses the traditional polarization between the United States and the other member states; provides a prospective bridge between the English-speaking and Ibero-American nations; and constitutes a power center in its own right.

These developments, plus the growing differentiations among the Latin American countries themselves, have dramatically changed the orientation of the OAS. In a real sense, OAS membership is now divided into five centers or groupings—the United States, Canada, the English-speaking Caribbean, the Rio Group (South America plus Mexico), and the smaller Latin states in Central America and the Caribbean. There are differences in outlook and tensions among them. The Rio Group calls itself "an international interlocutor,"[1] but some believe it aspires to be a major policy bloc. The group's coherence, however, is limited by some tensions within it and by lack of strong leadership. Mexico does not always agree with the Southern Cone countries; Brazil is still somewhat set apart by its potential for global reach, on the one hand, and the malaise created by its internal troubles on the other; and Venezuela's earlier leadership and influence have been weakened by Carlos Andres Pérez's departure.

As well as the resentments generated by asymmetry, cultural differences between the English-speaking Caribbean and the Latin American countries have been exacerbated by clashing views of OAS priorities. The Caribbean countries consider the OAS technical assistance program essential, and fear diversion of the organization's resources to other programs. Their tactical bloc voting is thus essentially a means of preserving their claims on resources and programs. Tension between the Caribbean and Rio groups has recently worsened.

With such a heterogenous membership, how can the OAS best function? What theorists call "hegemonic stability"—direction by one power or coalition of powers—is neither realistic nor acceptable today. The most frequently recommended alternative is one in which member states consult and coordinate with one other, forming ad hoc "steering caucuses" whose composition will differ depending on the subject at hand. This puts a premium, of course, on skilled and qualified representatives and on the "art" of multilateral diplomacy, which is quite distinct from bilateral diplomacy.

ORGANIZATIONAL PROLIFERATION. Beginning with the formation of the Special Committee for Latin American Coordination (CECLA) in 1969,[2] some of the hemisphere's nations have sought from time to time—especially during the past decade—to coordinate their policies and positions in order to deal with the United States (and the industrialized countries generally), as well as to advance their mutual interests. This has taken the form of a variety of organizations—subregional groupings like the Rio Group, the Organization of Eastern Caribbean States (OECS), and the Central American nations; subregional economic integration efforts such as the Southern Cone Free Market (MERCOSUR) and the Andean Pact; and regional entities like the Latin American Economic System (SELA), a purely Latin American economic forum into which CECLA was converted in 1973.

It would be unfortunate if such entities were perceived (or conceived of) as competitors or rivals of the OAS. On the contrary, there is considerable advantage in thinking of them as working parts of the larger regional mechanism. Subregional groupings or ad hoc arrangements, after all, may often be better able to act than the regional organization. The ability of the Central American states to finally broker peace in Nicaragua after more distant groups failed is a case in point. The principle of subsidiarity operates at this level no less than further up the scale. In any case, states will surely continue to make common cause, forming and re-forming groups to deal with their special interests.

Also proliferating and forming networks have been the independent, nongovernmental organizations (NGOs)—human rights groups, trade unions, professional and business associations, women's organizations, religious institutions, and environmental groups. These have contributed significantly to the maturation of civil society in the hemisphere. The potential for constructive cooperation and coordination between the NGOs and the OAS and its specialized agencies is certainly worth exploring.

None of this diversification should be surprising, given the complexity of issues and the congestion of players and interest groups on the international scene today. As Harlan Cleveland observed, international governance in the final years of the century is very likely to resemble a huge "global bazaar" in which actors at all levels are continuously engaged in parallel negotiations about strategically related but tactically separable matters.[3]

THE UN AND THE OAS. Today both the United Nations and the OAS have taken on renewed importance as governments strive to build a "new world order." Strikingly, both are grappling with debates over broadly similar conceptual and legal questions—intervention versus sovereignty, humanitarian and human rights cases, large versus small powers' interests, when the use of force is warranted. It is not surprising, therefore, that the question of the relationship between the two has increasingly attracted the attention of diplomats and government leaders.

In legal terms, the relationship is ambiguous.[4] It seems clear that the UN was never intended to be in every instance the court of first resort for conflicts and complaints. Article 52 of the UN Charter recognizes the existence of regional organizations and directs that they "make every effort" to resolve disputes. But it is not clear that this creates an obligation to refer problems to the regional organization before the UN steps in. Under Article 34, the Security Council may investigate any dispute or crisis threatening the peace, and Article 35 permits any member of the UN to bring any dispute to the attention of the Security Council or the General Assembly.

The Security Council can, under Chapter VII powers, impose binding sanctions, including the use of force, against a state that has breached or threatened the peace or committed aggression. This would seem to put the UN in the lead in peacemaking, since the OAS Charter has nothing similar in its provisions. Article 53 of the UN Charter permits the Security Council to use regional arrangements for enforcement action but prohibits regional enforcement without Security Council authorization. There has been no clear definition in practice, however, as to what sort of regional action is subject to Security Council consent, or under what conditions.

A case could perhaps be made that existing arrangements add up to a hierarchical system in which the OAS is part of the larger global body, but that view is not widely accepted in the hemisphere. Indeed, the dominant (but not unanimous) opinion among member states is that the two organizations are coequal, and that the relationship between them must be based on reciprocity and respect for the competencies and purposes of each. This point of view was stated most explicitly by OAS secretary-general Joao Baena Soares in remarks he presented in March 1993 to the United Nations Special Committee on the UN Charter and the Strengthening of the Organization:

> Cooperation between the OAS and the United Nations cannot be based on principles of hierarchy, for neither is dependent on or subordinate to the other. Nor may it be based on specialization, since both organizations are general in nature. To the contrary, it must recognize as its basis the community of purposes and principles between the two and the diversity of their competence. . . . Collaboration between the OAS and the United Nations is a relationship of mutual support and benefit between organizations that operate independently in two different spheres of competency. It is the diversity of their competencies that makes it possible for them to cooperate.[5]

The secretary-general went on to say that the OAS cannot be merely the executor of decisions made in the UN, nor is it appropriate for the world organization to say what activities regional organizations should engage in or what procedures they should adopt. In giving his reasons for these views, the secretary-general cited, among other things, the long history and traditions of the inter-American system. Latin American theorists have long maintained that a separate "inter-American" law and custom have developed out of that common heritage and experience applicable to intraregional relations among the member states, even though many of these precepts, such as democratic solidarity, are not yet recognized at the global level.

At the tactical and practical policy level, there are also conflicting arguments among OAS member states concerning the UN. Some argue that the overwhelming power of the United States can be diffused by using the UN forum. Others, particularly the small states, argue that bringing in the whole world only complicates problems, and that their own weight in the OAS is more significant than in the global organization. Some profess that regional, especially neighboring, powers have more knowledge with which to treat problems; others argue that neighbors may have axes to grind, and that a more distant organization might be more objective. Some governments are not prepared to submit decisions to the "great power" veto system of the Security Council. Others point out that the UN has more capacity and experience in dealing with peacekeeping, especially if armed units may be necessary. Several emphasize the advantage that the regional character of the OAS provides in its ability to adopt norms and obligations not possible on a global scale, citing the commitment to defend democracy as a case in point. There are, in addition, rivalries and turf jealousies between officials and staffs of the OAS and UN secretariats which are a hindrance to close cooperation.

A good example of the imprecision plaguing the global/regional relationship was the reaction of the two bodies to the military coup in Haiti on September 30, 1991.[6] Although the Security Council met late that same day at the request of the Haitian UN representative, it did not "formally" convene because a majority of the members felt that the coup was entirely a domestic matter beyond the competence of the Council. The OAS Permanent Council, however, obligated to act under Resolution 1080, met swiftly on September 30, condemned the coup, and convened an immediate Meeting of Consultation of Foreign Ministers, which met twice in eight days and, in effect, shaped the international response to the crisis. A subsequent meeting of the UN Security Council followed the OAS lead in rhetorically condemning the coup but adopted no formal resolution because China would not concur; in November 1991, the General Assembly passed a nonbinding resolution condemning the coup and urging support of the OAS-recommended embargo.

The circumstances surrounding the involvement of the UN in the Haitian case a year later further illustrates the complications of the UN/OAS relationship. It is safe to say that many of the Latin Americans, who had assumed that the OAS would continue to be the focal point for dealing with Haiti, were nonplussed at the parallel North American initiatives that suddenly expanded the OAS effort into a joint OAS/UN mediation process. This was especially true since, on December 13, 1992, almost simultaneously with the appointment of Dante Caputo as mediator, a Canadian proposal that the OAS seek the inscription of Haiti on the Security Council agenda was defeated, with the larger Latin American countries leading the opposition. (A compromise was approved subsequently, authorizing the OAS secretary-general to work closely with his UN counterpart.)[7] If the United States was now ready to use its leverage and step up the pressure on the Haitian parties to reach an agreement, many Latin Americans asked at the time, why did it not do so through the OAS, since the United States is the key actor and mover in both organizations anyway? More disturbingly, did the resort to the UN reflect a conscious or subconscious feeling among U.S. policymakers that the OAS is ineffective? Such a judgment would amount to a self-fulfilling prophecy.

When Caputo's mediation effort stalled, however, there was fairly wide tacit recognition that only UN enforcement measures under Chapter VII were likely to force the Haitian military to reach an agreement with Aristide. The result was a worldwide oil embargo decreed by the Security Council on June 25, 1993. Even then, Brazil, as a rotating member of the Security Council, led a successful effort to eliminate from the resolution an article that would have permitted a naval blockade to enforce the embargo, arguing that the use of military force was not justified in the circumstances.

Despite all the concern over appropriate roles, the OAS and the UN have, in fact, collaborated closely in the Haitian case. In addition to cooperation over the OAS/UN international civilian mission to Haiti already mentioned, there have been close consultations on planning for postagreement humanitarian and development aid for Haiti. It is therefore curious and unfortunate that the image projected by the U.S. media, contrary to the facts, has been that of a UN effort to "rescue" an ineffective OAS response. Seldom is the OAS ever mentioned in stories about the mediation and the agreement finally reached.

Aside from Haiti, there is a long record of collaboration and consultation between relevant agencies of the two organizations across a wide range of topics, especially the environment, narcotics, women's and indigenous people's contributions to development, and coordination of disaster relief.[8]

The Managua General Assembly instructed the Permanent Council to conduct a detailed study of relations between the two bodies and to formulate recommendations to be presented to the next assembly.[9] Many OAS members believe that the UN should manage its relationship with the OAS separately from the question of UN relations with other regional organizations. The OAS, they argue, is a unique regional entity because of its history, structure, and the singular fact that the United States is a full member. Many are very sensitive to any suggestion that the UN take the initiative in defining the relationship, as the OAS secretary-general's remarks testify. Both secretaries-general have supported a case-by-case approach as best for now, although both have called for an intensified pace of coordination and consultations.[10]

It would be lamentable and indeed unjustified if the various members came to see the UN and the OAS as rivals or competitors, or viewed the OAS itself as feckless and redundant. Both organizations, after all, have complementing strengths and capabilities. It would be far more helpful to think of the two in terms of a constructive symbiosis, a kind of conceptual "burden sharing." As trust and experience accumulate over time, more precise divisions of labor and jurisdiction will surely develop de facto. And that may turn out to be the real significance of Haiti.

THE FINANCIAL CONSTRAINT. The OAS is currently recovering from a serious financial crisis that brought the organization to the brink of bankruptcy in the 1980s. The crisis was triggered when the United States not only declined to pay its full assessment on time, allowing large arrearages to accumulate over the decade, but also decided unilaterally to reduce its share (66 percent) of total assessments. In 1990, the OAS approved a reduction in the U.S. quota; it now stands at 59.47 percent of total assessments. The United States has since resumed full payment of its current quota as well as some payments on its arrearages. At the end of 1992, however, the United States was still in arrears by $29.5 million.[11]

For the two-year budget period covering 1994 and 1995, the organization has called for a total assessment level (termed the "regular fund" budget) of $69 million, the U.S. share of which would be $41 million.[12] In addition to the regular fund, there is a "voluntary fund" covering contributions for technical assistance and related matters. Despite its name, these contributions are considered obligatory commitments. The annual level hoped for from this source is just under $24 million. Special contributions for specific programs and projects, such as the Nicaraguan CIAV/OAS mission, are an additional source of funds; such contributions have been made by individual member states as well as nonmember nations, including European countries and Japan, and international institutions, such as the Inter-American Development Bank. The contribution levels depend upon the projects and the circumstances. Much of the valuable work of the OAS, such as peacekeeping, CICAD, or the Unit for Democratic Development, depends on these contributions. The problem is that there is never certainty as to what payments will be received from any of these sources, even the quota assessments. The resulting precariousness in the organization's financing makes it difficult to plan with any predictability, or to adjust available funds to the organization's priorities.

In 1992, the actual program expenditures for technical assistance (not including managerial and administrative support costs) was $24 million, a slight increase over the previous two years.[13] As noted, the small countries, especially the Caribbean nations, consider this allocation vital, while the larger countries are less persuaded of its benefit. The question of allocating budget resources between technical assistance and the organization's other work is a matter of no small tension.

Clearly, the OAS cannot function without adequate financing. With needs growing for better OAS programs and services, the financial situation becomes a major constraint. There is a particular need for increased resources for the Unit for Democratic Development, peacekeeping and election observation missions, the Inter-American Human Rights Commission, and CICAD. The member states' interests in poverty relief, technical assistance, dealing with the environment, and general policy oversight all add to the demand. The economic strains and budgetary restrictions experienced by member states in their own domestic environment sharpen the agonies of the trade-offs. The OAS financial situation is truly a test of member states' commitment to regional governance; if they do not support it financially, it cannot be effective.

OPERATIONAL DILEMMAS

The OAS faces a series of interrelated dilemmas and tensions inherent in carrying out its mandate. The effectiveness of its future performance will depend in significant measure on how well the member states reconcile, adjust to, or accommodate these problems.

THE JURISDICTIONAL QUESTION. How to apply collective decisions, standards, and norms and at the same time observe the principles of nonintervention and sovereignty has always been a source of controversy in the OAS. The first point debated when the OAS takes up any specific situation is almost always: Does the organization have jurisdiction?

The jurisdictional dilemma is embedded in the wording of the Charter itself. Articles 18 and 19 flatly bar any interference in the domestic affairs of member states. Yet other articles, treaties (such as the American Convention on Human Rights), and documents (for example, the Santiago Commitment) create obligations in the areas of human rights, support for democracy, and dispute settlement, all of which establish a collective interest in the internal behavior of a state and implicitly limit the meaning of sovereignty. While Article 16 of the Charter, for example, affirms each state's right "to develop its cultural, political and economic life freely and naturally," it also specifies that "in this free development, the State shall respect the rights of the individual and the principle of universal morality." Article 22 specifically exempts from the provisions of Article 18 "measures adopted for the maintenance of peace and security in accordance with existing treaties." And Article 60 permits the convening of Meetings of Consultation of Foreign Ministers (see Appendix 4) to consider "problems of an urgent nature and of common interest"—with no other qualification specified. The ambiguities and contradictions in the basic documents and treaties thus provide considerable leeway for varied interpretations and judgments.

The transformations wrought by turbulence and change in the world have intensified this tension between collective (OAS or UN) jurisdiction and a state's sovereignty. Today, very few domestic matters are without an international dimension, and internal crises are with growing frequency portrayed as a threat to international peace. The world's expanding humanitarian concerns and the hemisphere's emphasis on democratic systems provide new legal weight to the rights of individuals as opposed to the rights of states. Economic integration, which in the Western Hemisphere is politically fashionable and earnestly sought after, challenges the concept of national sovereignty by definition.

There are, in short, increasing areas of interstate relations in which the boundaries that divide the affairs of states from those of collective jurisdiction are no longer clear-cut. As the UN secretary-general observed, "The time of absolute and exclusive sovereignty . . . has passed; its theory was never matched by reality. It is the task of leaders of States today to understand this and to find a balance between the needs of good internal governance and the requirements of an ever more interdependent world."[14]

PROBLEM SOLVING OR RELIANCE ON LEGAL SAFEGUARDS. Differing historical experiences and cultural perspectives between the United States and Latin America affect the way each conceptualizes the end purpose of the OAS. U.S. thinking about the OAS has shifted since the end of the cold war from the traditional notion of a security alliance to one that sees collective problem solving as its central purpose. In this view, legal principles and concepts, while important, are not static but modifiable by collective agreements, precedents, and new circumstances. The pragmatism of the U.S. national character is partly at the root of this conception, but it is also a "great power" mind-set. As political theorists have noted, big powers do not worry too much about outside intervention (from which their power protects them), but are more motivated by the Thucydidean notion that a big power simply does what it thinks it needs to do to advance its interests.

Latin American countries, on the other hand, are passionately concerned with the safeguards of international legal principles and doctrine. These are, after all, their major defenses against the "great powers," especially the United States. In this view, problem solving is subject to the limits imposed by the "rules" of international law. Although often criticized by U.S. commentators as overly legalistic or a Latin proclivity to accept form over substance, the Latin American perspective is deeper than that. It reflects what one might call a "bill of rights" mind-set. That is to say, the safeguard against abuse of power is primary, and any breach of that safeguard, however seemingly justified in the concrete instance, is unacceptable.[15]

Robert Hunter's comment on the recent UN mission to restore order and end starvation in Somalia is a particularly apt description of the view of many Latin American countries on just this point:

> The idea of breaching sovereignty for broader purpose
> needs to develop a significant pedigree before it can be
> pronounced to be truly sound. Defining the limits of
> intervention and the aspects of sovereignty that still
> need to be preserved in the common interest has yet
> to be done. Until it is, a proper desire to expand the
> rule of law risks becoming an excuse to impose a polit-
> ical preference on other countries that will be stoutly
> resisted both by them and by others fearing for their
> own independence.[16]

This explains why Latin American states always qualify their agreement to collective enterprises with such phrases as "with due respect for the principles of self-determination and non-intervention." The United States, conversely, usually qualifies its commitment to collective arrangements with the caveat that it reserves the option of unilateral action.[17] These two perspectives are not irreconcilable, but each side needs to accurately comprehend and appreciate the viewpoint of the other.

DECISIONMAKING: VOTING VERSUS CONSENSUS. International organizations like the UN and the OAS often face a contentious choice between acting decisively and acting inclusively. When the United Nations was founded, the determination was made that decisionmaking had to reflect the distribution of power among the member states. Thus, the locus of UN enforcement activity, concentrated in the Security Council, was designed to allow the great powers, the "permanent five," to veto unilaterally measures not to their liking. The General Assembly operates on the basis of one state, one vote, but its resolutions are not binding.

In the case of the OAS, on the other hand, the trade-off came to favor mutual accord. The history and asymmetrical nature of the U.S.-Latin American relationship made a decisionmaking process based on power distribution unacceptable. Hence the principle underlying the Charter is the juridical equality of states. Running counter to U.S. hegemony in the hemisphere, there gradually developed over time a tradition and practice of reaching substantive decisions by consensus, even though the Charter contemplated decisions by vote.

The conviction is now strong among the OAS member states that decision by consensus is the best way to ensure that in the long run expressed values and principles will take force. The need to reach consensus does, as an empirical matter, tend to force the members to negotiate and renegotiate decisions and "bring everyone along." In fact, the process has resulted in significant, if cautious, movement toward agreement on principles and guidelines covering an impressive number of topics from the environment to human rights.

Critics of the consensus process argue that it delays decisions and dilutes effectiveness—especially to the extent that smaller countries' interests diverge from the mainstream—and, in essence, invites frustrated stronger members to take matters into their own hands. That has happened, as in the case of the U.S. invasion of Panama in 1989, but such adventures simply compound the fear smaller member states have of unilateral dominance. Yet in the face of such problems as Haiti, and with other danger signs emanating from the serious internal situation in Cuba, the feeling is growing that perhaps the organization needs to improve both the speed and the effectiveness of its decisions. Sooner or later the members may feel compelled to reopen the voting/consensus debate.[18]

PEACEKEEPING AND THE USE OF FORCE. The inter-American system has a long tradition of peacefully resolving interstate conflict that antedates the OAS.[19] Through use of a wide variety of settlement patterns—mediation, good offices, arbitration—some ad hoc, some by regional mechanisms, the region has historically been one of the most peaceful in the world in terms of interstate conflict. The respectable dispute-settlement record of the OAS itself has already been noted.

In recent years, and particularly since 1990, the OAS has with growing frequency sought to assist in the settlement of internal conflict and crises, which are increasingly viewed as threats to the hemisphere's peace and solidarity. These efforts have encompassed the variety of activities previously described, such as election observation missions, fact-finding, and mediation (as in Guatemala); internal verification and monitoring of peace agreements (as in Nicaragua and Suriname); monitoring of ongoing political processes and commitments (as in the case of Peru); and observation and reporting on human rights conditions. All of these activities, it should be emphasized, have consisted of *unarmed civilian teams*, as distinguished from similar United Nations missions, which frequently use military contingents authorized to defend themselves if conflict resumes or breaks out.

Up to now OAS peacekeeping efforts have been based squarely on the principle of consent, that is, mediating and persuading the parties concerned to reach agreement among themselves, and inserting verification and monitoring missions only with the acquiesence of all sides. The case of Haiti, however, has posed a dilemma: Should the OAS also be prepared to compel resolution of a dispute or enforcement of an internal agreement? The challenge can be stated even more broadly: Should the OAS develop a collective capacity to use coercion, including the use of force if necessary, for broad collective security purposes— not only in cases of aggression but to restore democracy, to bring hostile parties to an agreement, to attend to humanitarian or human rights emergencies or other serious threats to the region's peace?

Interestingly, the use of force has become a controversial question in the United Nations arena as well. Even though the UN Charter legally permits the use of force, questions of both a practical and ethical nature have been raised about when and how that should be done. The frustrations of war in Bosnia and the violence imperiling the Somalia famine relief effort have added to the quandary. Conceptually, is the option to use force if peaceful means fail essential to the credibility and success of a peacekeeping regime, as the UN secretary-general argues? Or is it perilous to encourage "tendencies favorable to the use of force" whatever the grounds, as the OAS secretary-general has argued? [20]

The dilemma and the governing circumstances are, of course, considerably different in nature at the hemispheric and the global levels. Unlike the UN Charter, it is unclear that there is any legal basis in the OAS Charter for the use of force, or for that matter even for obligatory sanctions. Decisions on sanctions by the Permanent Council or Meetings of Foreign Ministers are not binding, and are usually phrased as recommendations. Proposals have been made, however, calling on member states to put in place domestic legislation that would permit prompt compliance with such recommendations. Second, there is the historical and deep-seated fear among OAS member governments that granting any legitimacy to the use of force for peacekeeping purposes might be used by the United States or the larger Latin American powers to impose their political preferences on the domestic affairs of others.

The resolution of this particular dilemma may perhaps lie in some coordinated division of labor with the United Nations in which, if force seems justified, resort could be made to the UN's Chapter VII powers, as occurred in the case of the Haiti oil embargo. In his comments to the UN Special Committee on the United Nations Charter, however, OAS secretary-general Baena Soares provocatively contrasted the roles of the two organizations in words that, though his own personal view, probably also reflect the predominant opinion among member governments:

> The Organization of American States and the United Nations are expressions of different motivations on the part of the States that founded them. The world organization exists first and foremost to avert war and to watch over and maintain international peace, whereas the OAS was established to strengthen hemispheric solidarity. . . . Article 1 of the OAS Charter states that the Organization has no powers other than those expressly conferred upon it by the Charter itself. No provision authorizes the use of force by the Organization save in the express exception of external aggression. With that exception, therefore, the use of force has no legitimacy in the legal framework that governs relations among the American States. . . . Proscription of the use of force within the Organization of American States is not at odds with the purpose of strengthening peace and security in the hemisphere. The peaceful procedures adopted for this purpose are ways that the region has chosen for itself and do not affect the stringent restrictions on the legitimate use of force in effect in the international system. In permitting the legitimate use of force to maintain peace and security, the international community has given the United Nations functions and means that are effectively controlled only at that level. . . . It would be perilous to encourage tendencies favorable to the use of force—even in exceptional situations—whatever the grounds on which it could be resorted to.[21]

Whatever may develop in the UN/OAS relationship, the following seems to be the current common denominator of agreement among OAS member states on the subject of peacekeeping:

▲ Diplomatic and economic sanctions may be recommended, but the use of military force will not be considered.

▲ OAS military contingents for protection as part of peacekeeping missions is a controversial subject, and probably not "doable" now.

▲   It should be made clear that overthrowing a democratic
    government will not be cost-free, but there is not much
    agreement on how to determine what price the aggres-
    sors should pay.

CENTRALIZE OR DEPUTIZE. Should member states seek to establish a more
professional and centralized mechanism or process vested in the OAS
itself to deal with the problems of conflict management and peacekeeping? Or should it simply authorize members, individually or collectively, to do so?

It is relevant to this discussion to note that the United Nations con-
fronts a somewhat similar problem regarding the use of force as specified in Chapter VII of its Charter. Giving the UN a military capacity
under its own control has been recommended by Secretary-General
Boutros Boutros-Ghali. As yet, however, UN members have not been
willing to establish a standing force or to designate standby units for
UN missions.[22] Instead, in crises the UN has had to rely on the offers of
member states to do the job, as in the cases of the Korean War, the
Persian Gulf War, and the Somalia famine relief.

With no consensus on the use of force in the OAS, neither a standing inter-American peace force nor the advance designation of standby
units is at the moment a realistic possibility, or even under discussion.
The OAS has by and large met requirements for conflict resolution and
dispute settlement ad hoc, designating special negotiating or mediating
missions, or drawing on member states' officials, as in the cases of Haiti,
Peru, and Guatemala.

There have been some efforts to build an in-house capacity for such
things as observer and monitoring missions, fact-finding and election-
monitoring tasks, but much more could be done. Reinforcing and further professionalizing the Unit for Democratic Development would be
a logical course to follow. A number of proposals have, in fact, been
made to give the unit an "early warning" capability to gather and analyze information where political unrest or violence may be impending
and a capacity to formulate strategy for meeting an imminent threat to
democratic rule or to the peace in general, or for restoring peace or
democratic rule after the event. This could be accomplished either by
developing an internal cadre with such expertise or by earmarking a
standing group of outside experts on which the secretary-general or
the Permanent Council could draw.

Such proposals would not be easy to implement, however, considering the organization's long history of fiscal undernourishment and
staffing problems. Like any bureaucracy, that of the OAS is shaped by

long-standing habits, which make it prone to reaction rather than activism and predisposed to do only what it believes the members will allow. There is also some tension between staffing for ability and staffing for political reasons, such as patronage or filling country quotas.

As an abstract proposition, there is logic in authorizing those nations with the resources to do so to implement the organization's decisions, since many members may lack the capacity to participate in joint action. Similarly, offers to take the lead are often necessary "as a catalyst for broader involvement," as President Bush put it with reference to Somalia.[23]

Such deputizing, however, is unlikely to become a common practice. In any major peacemaking activity, the United States would clearly be the key actor, and fear that the OAS might become simply a vehicle for the United States is still of real concern for many. In words that are probably interchangeable with the views of a number of Western Hemisphere nations about the OAS, UN secretary-general Boutros-Ghali observed in a recent interview: "Just as the United States doesn't like others to take charge, other countries also don't like the United States to play a dominant role in the United Nations. . . . The image will come to be that the United Nations equals the United States, and then many nations will no longer accept the UN."[24]

The point to be reiterated is that the legitimacy of collective actions rests squarely on consensus. This is especially relevant in the case of the OAS, but it applies to the UN as well. As consensus on the norms and principles regarding collective security, peacekeeping, dispute settlement, or any cooperative programs develops and expands, so does the legitimacy of both that consensus and the organization itself. This underlines the importance to the OAS of the consensus-building process. As compelling as the problem-solving impulse might seem in any given case, before taking actions that risk shattering or weakening the regional consensus member states need to give the most careful consideration to the possible long-term damage to the larger goal of creating an effective international organization.

CHAPTER 5

CONCLUSIONS AND ASSESSMENT

A uniquely auspicious climate for hemispheric cooperation exists today, presenting a historic—but passing—opportunity to revitalize the OAS. While the particular circumstances for which the OAS was originally created have changed over time, its underlying raison d'etre has remained powerful. It is still the only place where all the countries of the hemisphere can meet with a regional focus on regional policy and mutual problems; none of the myriad other organizations and subregional arrangements can fully replace it. With the world's dynamics moving toward greater international interdependence—especially in the Western Hemisphere—the need for a pan-American forum to deal with matters of vital interest to all is now greater than ever. Moreover, because the United States is itself more aware than ever of the impact of its hemispheric ties, developing the OAS into an effective instrument of regional governance is clearly of major importance to the U.S. national interest.

Looking back at inter-American relations since the end of World War II, it is clear that a good many of the region's current attitudes and principles can be traced to debates held and decisions taken through the OAS. The OAS was a vehicle for spreading awareness of the importance of human rights, and for the creation of mechanisms to defend and promote them, earlier than in most other parts of the world. The region's aspirations for social and economic development were greatly energized and shaped by the Alliance for Progress, and much of the growth in the region's institutional capacities in the development field was the direct consequence of OAS activity in the Inter-American Committee for the Alliance for Progress (CIAP). It was the OAS that enabled the member states to make democracy a regional principle and its violation grounds for collective action. In sum, hemisphere affairs would certainly have been different—and probably much worse—if the OAS had not been created in 1948.

A closely related observation is that the OAS has performed far better than most people in the United States think—especially in dispute settlement and peacekeeping. The U.S. public (and even the scholarly community) is generally unaware of the significant role the OAS played in Nicaragua, Suriname, and Haiti. Curiously, the U.S. media almost never mention the OAS at all, whereas in the other nations of the region, information about the OAS and what it does is frequent and prominent fare. The OAS—and the UN, for that matter—is an instrument of the states that formed it. There is an unfortunately widespread habit among many people to respond to the frustrations of intractable problems by an almost reflexive appeal—like an incantation—to "The" OAS or "The" UN, as if these organizations somehow possess autonomous power and capabilities. But, of course, they do not. They are neither a deus ex machina nor a self-executing mechanism like the World Bank. They can be no more or less than the member states want them to be.

It is unrealistic to think that the member states will make huge changes suddenly, sharply transforming both the OAS and the region's dynamics. Pragmatically, the best chance for development of the OAS lies in incrementalism: small gains, modest shifts in attitude, and cumulative processes that add up over time to substantial advances. As the hemisphere nations learn to work with the OAS and channel more and more of their interlocking relationships through it, they will gain both experience and reassurance in the process. The OAS could conceivably become a more determinative organization, an agent as well as a product of change.

In comparing the normative and juridical bases on which the organization now operates with those of twenty years ago, it is clear that the OAS has—cautiously but noticeably—widened agreement as to what principles ought to govern states' behavior across a range of issues. It has become, in that sense, a real source of legitimacy for governments. The assertion of democratic values and the rights of individuals are obvious examples, but the OAS has expanded discussion and produced accord in other areas as well. In June 1991, the 21st General Assembly approved the first ever "action plan" for environmental protection, enumerating steps that should be undertaken by individual states and cooperative regional efforts.[1] Consensus building, especially in terms of reinterpreting traditional precepts and legal concepts, promises to be the soundest long-term route to the development of regimes for environmental and other issues that cross state borders.

Having made reasonable progress in building consensus, member states are now forced to grapple with the consequences: What is the extent of their collective responsibility to carry out and defend the norms they proclaim? The OAS has, throughout its history, demonstrated some ad hoc capacities for collective action. Its mediation and dispute settlement functions and the activities of the Unit for Democratic Development are cases in point. But today the need is for much more systematic capabilities. Without further progress in that direction, consensus building risks degenerating into a mere exercise in hortatory rhetoric.

Even where there is a broad sharing of basic values and goals, member states still differ among themselves as to just what that means for the OAS in terms of specific roles and functions. A few would prefer that it be little more than a forum for debates and discussion. Others believe that its ability to act as a collective should be carefully circumscribed and controlled by the members. Still others are prepared to vest some power and authority in the organization to act as the region's agent for joint management of problems that cannot be handled adequately any other way.

This difference of opinion puts a premium on diplomacy, dialogue, and shared learning. It means honestly recognizing the nature of basic fears and concerns about sovereignty and nonintervention, and the depth of the reflexive suspicions about U.S. motives and intentions that exist in Latin America. Precisely because the OAS is the instrument of the members, efforts need to be made to build support for the OAS within individual states and to make the concepts, ideals, and goals of regional governance attractive to national leaders and the broad public. Unless the countries of Latin America and the Caribbean feel they have a real stake in the system, and unless they feel assured that the United States will use its power responsibly and with restraint, the organization will not flourish.

One core task, surely, is to reconcile the tension between those who want the organization to be primarily a means to problem solving and those who stress the application of legal safeguards. A suggestion concerning what might be done would be for the Inter-American Juridical Committee, the organization's advisory body on juridical matters (see Appendix 4), to sponsor a long-term policy study of the sovereignty/interdependence, intervention/nonintervention tensions in the twenty-first century, involving political theorists and legal experts from Europe, Asia, and North America as well as Latin America and the Caribbean. Such a project might, at a minimum, improve mutual understanding of different views. At a maximum, it might very well help shape the nature of an emergent new world order.

It is striking that so many inquiries into the OAS by U.S. writers and scholars focus on internal structural and procedural reform—or on new programmatic activities—as the key to improving its effectiveness, without any realistic appraisal of the recommendations' prospects and with relatively little attention given to the policies, interests, and fears of the individual member states. Usually phrased with hortatory "shoulds" and "musts," such proposals' validity almost always depends on the assumption that all member states see the objective, goal, and purpose in the same way, and that it is just a question of the best means. But that is seldom the case.

This is not to disparage recommendations for internal reforms. Streamlining and rationalizing procedures, upgrading the quality and expertise of staffs, and devising imaginative new activities are all ultimately essential to improved performance. The role of the secretary-general, for example, offers a special potential for generating new ideas, innovative management, and strategies, even though the Charter—and the member states—have placed considerable restraints on what the secretary-general can do. Now, more than ever, it is essential for member governments to understand and appreciate the importance of this position and the qualities the incumbent must possess, since the organization will elect a new secretary-general in March 1994 for a five-year term.

The point to be emphasized in all this is that reforms follow political consensus. In the words of one scholar, the failures and inadequacies of multilateral institutions almost always stem from "lack of political consensus and not organizational malfunction."[2] It is, in short, political will that produces organizational and programmatic changes, not the other way around.

A somewhat different approach—looking at the OAS from the standpoint of the member states—is to ask what opportunities are present for the OAS to become the principal channel through which member states take action? For what aspects of inter-American affairs is the OAS the most suitable instrument for individual member governments to pursue their interests? These questions require contemplation of priorities, comparative advantage, and where the OAS might optimally concentrate its attentions.

The hemisphere's nations are intensely concerned today with the interconnected objectives of promoting and defending democracy, advancing and protecting human rights, improving security, and effective peacekeeping and conflict resolution. As already noted, the OAS is the only regionwide mechanism available to the member states for such cooperative action. These political objectives, moreover, are enshrined in the Charter as essential to hemispheric solidarity. All this suggests that the priority in directing and focusing the OAS should be given to such political functions.

In other major areas of concern, such as economics, trade, and environment, there is a surfeit of international organizations and a variety of functioning channels, both multilateral and subregional. The OAS is thus unlikely to occupy center stage when governments deal with such questions. But there is still a need for some way to oversee and broadly relate these issues to political and social goals like democracy and security. The OAS is a fitting panregional instrument for that purpose. The Permanent Council could quite appropriately serve as a coordinating body following policy developments and providing guidance and recommendations to both member governments and international institutions. Policy oversight is, in short, a second suitable priority for OAS specialization.

The variety of special services and assistance provided by a myriad of specialized agencies, committees, and commissions suggests a third priority. The governing bodies of the OAS—the three Councils (the Permanent Council, CIES, and CIECC) and the Secretariat—have never decided to what extent they should themselves engage in program execution as distinct from policy guidance, or how much to centralize operations under their direct control or decentralize to specialized entities. Different patterns have been followed by different bodies at different times. A more optimal use of OAS energies would be a "linchpin" concept,[3] that is, decentralizing operational matters (such as technical assistance, narcotics, etc.) to its subsidiary agencies, commissions, or committees (such as CICAD, the Inter-American Human Rights Commission, the Pan American Health Organization), while the central governing bodies concentrate on overall policy control and coordination. In this concept, the councils and the secretary-general's office would constitute the coordinating hub of a flexible array of decentralized, associated, and even independent organizations and cooperative ventures. This linchpin role would be an especially useful way for member governments to ensure coordination among agencies, including those with a global reach, involved in hemispheric affairs.

In the final analysis, the future prospects of the OAS will be shaped to a substantial degree by the United States. This country cannot by itself make the OAS effective nor determine how the organization is to function. Indeed, for the United States to presume to design a blueprint to make the OAS an effective multilateral institution would amount to a contradiction in terms. No one in the hemisphere really disputes that U.S. influence and willingness to use its resources to carry out OAS decisions are essential and would be a powerful catalyst to broader regionwide attempts at collective governance. What arouses concern in Latin America and the Caribbean are the intentions, style, and "hegemonic" proclivities of U.S. involvement. This is understandable. The United States has always had trouble committing itself to any multilateral arrangements or policies it did not effectively control, or allowing others to share in the determination of its policies.

If the United States thinks of the OAS as its alliance; if Americans fall back into the "exceptionalist" habit of projecting their interpretations, experience, and objectives as universal and good for all; if the "can do" quality of their nature leads them to throw their weight around; if this nation expects others to essentially accept its schemes but is unwilling to adjust to theirs, then it will surely resurrect old resentments and recalcitrance and shatter consensus. If, on the other hand, U.S. policymakers honestly consult and discuss, listen and bargain, convey mutual respect and consideration, the result could be an exemplary regional organization. There is a subtle but crucial difference between using power and influence to lead, nudge, and cajole and the arrogance of assuming that that power entitles the possessor to direct and prescribe. U.S. policy makers would do well to remember that Latin America responded positively to the Enterprise for the Americas Initiative in good part because it was presented not as a blueprint but as an idea to be negotiated and worked out together.

There are four immediate actions that the Clinton administration would do well to consider:

1. Prompt, high-level consultations with individual hemispheric governments with three objectives in mind: a) to build support among the countries for the concept of truly multilateral cooperation to deal with regional problems; b) to make clear that the United States takes the OAS seriously as a major instrument for carrying out that concept, and to assure other countries of our full and constructive cooperation in the organization's work; and c) to obtain other governments' views on how to improve OAS effectiveness, what priorities to establish, and how to proceed over the near term.

2. On the basis of information gleaned in these consultations, formulation of a systematic U.S. policy toward the OAS: goals and objectives to be sought, strategies and game plans to achieve them. Without such a conscious effort, opportunities

will be lost and the OAS could easily slip back to being an afterthought for policymakers, as it often has in the past. In this regard, there are three sectors in particular in which effective OAS performance would be very much in the U.S. interest and for which U.S. ideas, influence, and support are critical:

▲ Programs and incentives to strengthen democracy and prevent democratic breakdowns. Professionalizing and reinforcing the Unit for Democratic Development, as suggested earlier, is an example of immediate steps that could be taken.

▲ Strengthened resources and mandate for the Inter-American Human Rights Commission.

▲ Cooperative programs in the security area to promote confidence-building measures, strengthen arms limitation and arms control programs, and improve civil-military relations. The agenda that the organization's Special Committee on Hemispheric Security has been developing is a convenient and ready-made framework for early action.

It will also be important for U.S. policymakers to prepare their positions carefully for the Special Session of the General Assembly on Inter-American Cooperation on Development, referred to earlier, which is to be held in Mexico in early 1994. To the Latin American and Caribbean countries economic and social development are the most crucial elements in preserving democracy, and they attach great importance to the Mexico meeting. This may be an area where it is more difficult for the United States to be responsive, but if the U.S. posture is perceived as passive, uninterested, or worse, as foot-dragging, much of the old recrimination will resurface.

3. Elimination of U.S. financial arrears owed to the organization as soon as possible, and consultations with both the secretary-general and member states as to how to ensure adequate financing for the future.

4. Pressure for prompt Senate ratification of a) the pending Charter reforms—the Protocols of Cartagena (pending since

1985), Washington, and Managua; b) the American Convention on Human Rights; and c) the Headquarters Agreement signed between the United States and the OAS on May 15, 1992, which outlines the privileges, immunities, and status governing the organization's operations on U.S. territory. (Unlike the case of the United Nations, no legal instrument has ever defined these matters with regard to OAS property and staff; the agreement is meant to regularize the legal status and define rights and obligations as in the case of the UN.) No better signal could be given that the United States takes the OAS seriously than quick action on these pending treaties.

A final cautionary note is in order. I have stressed that a number of conceptual differences, dilemmas, and tensions confront the OAS and its member states. To overcome these hurdles, the nations of the hemisphere need to formulate clear goals, establish well-defined norms, and rehabilitate existing mechanisms and procedures. Their chances of doing so successfully will depend ultimately upon shared basic values. The progress of the last three years has rested precisely on such shared values, particularly on the importance of democratic political systems, human rights, and liberal economic models. What is unclear, however, is just how deep or permanent the various nations' commitment to such principles really is. Certainly, democracy has not been consolidated throughout the region. The pressures of poverty and pent-up demand for social services put both democratic systems and liberal macroeconomic policies very much at risk. Observance of human rights is still very uneven throughout the region. The international situation itself is in turmoil. Global dynamics do not always evolve in ways that could be considered beneficial, and states can be propelled to increasingly self-centered and narrow interpretations of national interests.

It is entirely possible for the OAS to become an effective instrument of regional governance, capable of coping with transnational problems and dangers. But there is no certainty that the region's nations will be purposeful or enlightened enough to make those efforts successful. What *is* certain, however, is that there has never been a more propitious moment to try.

NOTES

INTRODUCTION

1. The phrase is the title of an essay on the dramatic changes in the world by Robert Tucker in Nicholas Rizopoulos, ed., *Sea Changes: U.S. Foreign Policy in a World Transformed* (New York: Council on Foreign Relations, 1990), p. 204. A shorter version appears in *Foreign Affairs* 69, no. 4 (Fall 1990).

2. The word "regime" appears in the sense that that term is used in current political science literature, that is, as arrangements and sets of norms, rules, principles, and procedures that operate in particular issue areas to guide the interactions of relevant actors (states as well as transnational entities). Stephen D. Krasner, ed., *International Regimes* (Ithaca, N.Y.: Cornell University Press, 1983).

CHAPTER 1

1. John Lewis Gaddis, "Toward the Post Cold War World," *Foreign Affairs* 70, no. 2 (Spring 1991): 103.

2. See, for example, Henry Kissinger, "False Dreams of a New World Order," *Washington Post*, February 26, 1991, and Owen Harries, "Fourteen Points for Realists," *The National Interest*, Winter 1992/1993, pp. 109–12. For a discussion of the debate as to whether the realist paradigm is still adequate, see James Rosenau, *Turbulence in World Politics: A Theory of Change and Continuity* (Princeton, N.J.: Princeton University Press, 1990). See especially Chapters 5 and 10.

3. See Rosenau, *Turbulence in World Politics*.

4. For this point, I am indebted to Terry Deibel. See his essay, "Strategies Before Containment," *International Security* 16, no. 4 (Spring 1992): 86. He also quotes Innis Claude, "For the balance of power system is not one which exists

only if instituted by deliberate choice; rather, it is the system which exists unless and until superseded by a consciously erected alternative."

5. See, for example, *Making the World Safe for America: A U.S. Foreign Policy Blue Print* (Washington, D.C.: Heritage Foundation, 1992), p. 27. Peter Rodman, currently a fellow at the Johns Hopkins University's Foreign Policy Institute and a former NSC official, distinguishes between what he calls genuine or "muscular" multilateralism and "mushy" multilateralism. The latter "makes deference to the international consensus almost an end in itself," discourages any unilateral American action, and sometimes becomes "an excuse for inaction." Muscular multilateralism, on the other hand, recognizes the continued relevance of power "in its very classical form," and "understands that American leadership can shape the international consensus." U.S. Institute of Peace, "Alternative U.S. Policy Approaches to Third World Conflict," *In Brief*, no. 24, Washington, D.C., January 1991.

6. For the most concise formulation of the "unipolar world" view, see Charles Krauthammer, "The Unipolar Moment," *Foreign Affairs* 70, no. 1 (1990–1991): 23–33. See also Harries, "Fourteen Points for Realists," and *Making the World Safe for America*. For a typical statement of the "U.S. interests first" position, see Alan Tonelson, "What Is the National Interest?" *Atlantic Monthly*, July 1991, pp. 35–52; and "Superpower without a Sword," *Foreign Affairs* 72, no. 3 (Summer 1993): 166–80.

7. James N. Rosenau, "Normative Challenges in a Turbulent World," *Ethics and International Affairs*, 6 (1992): 3, published annually by the Carnegie Council on Ethics and International Affairs.

CHAPTER 2

1. I use the term "inter–American system" to mean the loose conglomeration of intergovernmental organizations that link the hemisphere through a wide range of issues and functions. I think it is not practically useful to debate whether the inter-American system is a "system" in the sense discussed in international relations theory.

2. For a history of the early years of the inter-American system, see M. Margaret Ball, *The OAS in Transition* (Durham, N.C.: Duke University Press, 1969), and O. Carlos Stoetzer, *The Organization of American States*, 2d ed. (New York: Praeger, 1993).

3. L. Ronald Scheman, *The Inter-American Dilemma* (New York: Praeger, 1988), p. 3.

4. These included the Inter-American Conference in Montevideo (1933), Buenos Aires (1936), and Lima (1938); the resolutions adopted in three Meetings of Foreign Ministers: Panama (1939), Havana (1940), and Rio de Janeiro (1942); and the Act of Chapultepec (1945). For a summary of the modern collective

security aspects of the system, see David Painter, "Collective Security and the Inter-American System," Department of State Publication no. 9511, Office of the Historian, November 1986. See also Jorge Domínguez, "Political Relations in the Western Hemisphere," in *Governance in the Western Hemisphere*, ed. Viron P. Vaky (New York: Praeger, 1983), pp. 135–58.

5. The "bargain" had been adumbrated by the acceptance de jure by Franklin Roosevelt of the principle of nonintervention in the agreements reached in Montevideo (1933) and Buenos Aires (1936). See Scheman, *The Inter-American Dilemma*, Chapter 1, and Domínguez, "Political Relations in the Western Hemisphere," pp. 136–42.

6. For a discussion of disputes handled by the OAS, see Scheman, *The Inter-American Dilemma*, pp. 51–102. See also Joseph S. Nye, Jr., *Peace in Parts: Integration and Conflict in Regional Organizations* (Boston: Little, Brown and Co., 1971), pp. 129–54. It is fair to note that most of the disputes that the OAS was called upon to resolve took place in the Caribbean and Central America. Many of the South American conflicts, like the Argentine/Chilean territorial conflict over the Beagle Channel in Tierra del Fuego, were settled by ad hoc arrangements or submission to other mediators and arbiters.

7. For an account and analysis of the Alliance for Progress, see Jerome Levinson and Juan de Onis, *The Alliance That Lost Its Way: A Critical Report on the Alliance for Progress* (Chicago: Quadrangle Books, 1970).

8. The Nicaraguan elections were also monitored, as discussed later in the text, by missions from the UN and the European Community, as well as numerous private groups. The most prominent of the latter was a delegation chaired by former president Jimmy Carter representing the Council of Freely Elected Heads of Government, an organization of former Western Hemisphere chief executives sponsored and supported by the Carter Center, Emory University. For an account of that group's observation mission as well as background on the Council itself, see *Observing Nicaragua's Elections, 1989–1990*, Special Report no. 1, The Carter Center, Atlanta, 1990.

9. Bolivia and Paraguay have already held presidential elections in 1993. Chile and Venezuala are also scheduled to hold general elections this year. Countries scheduled to hold elections in 1994 are Brazil, Colombia, Costa Rica, the Dominican Republic, El Salvador, Honduras, Mexico, and Panama. Argentina, Guatemala, Peru, and Uruguay will hold elections in 1995.

CHAPTER 3

1. These topics are obviously interrelated: economic development and combating poverty are crucial to the maintenance of democracy; environmental concerns and the narcotics problem are relevant to a redefinition of security; economic integration and scientific/educational exchanges are important to economic

development. This agenda was reconfirmed in the "Declaration of Nassau" approved by the 22d General Assembly. AG/doc 2849/92 rev 1, May 19, 1992.

2. *Protocol of Amendment to the Charter of the Organization of American States, "Protocol of Managua,"* signed in Managua, Nicaragua, June 10, 1993. Reforms to the Charter are technically treaties, and are always termed "Protocol" and identified by the name of the city in which the protocol was approved.

3. A full history and analysis of CECON is contained in Martha Lynch, "Las relaciones comerciales entre América Latina y el Caribe y los Estados Unidos vistas a través de la Comisión Especial de Consulta y Negociación de la O.E.A.: Lecciones para el futuro," paper published (DT-CHO-26) in the series of Working Documents on Trade in the Western Hemisphere published jointly by the Inter-American Development Bank and the UN Economic Commission for Latin America and the Caribbean, February 1993.

4. OEA/Ser. P, AG/doc 2984/93, rev 1, June 11, 1993.

5. "Given the seriousness of the economic and social development problems facing the countries of Latin America and the Caribbean, the OAS, being the political forum that it is, must play a leading role in inter-American dialogue and cooperation so as to overcome current problems and redirect the area's general development. . . . The OAS, the only one that can serve as a forum of dialogue for all parties involved, should become for Latin America and the Caribbean, the United States and Canada, the political arena for the EAI." *Report of the Group of Consultation on the Inter-American System,* OEA/Ser. P, AG/CP/doc 516/91, April 24, 1991. As mandated by the 20th General Assembly, the secretary-general appointed a high-level independent Group of Consultation to examine the future of hemisphere relations and of the OAS and to report to the Permanent Council.

6. *Protocol of Amendment to the Charter of the Organization of American States, "Protocol of Washington,"* signed in Washington, D.C., December 14, 1992.

7. OEA/Ser. P, AG/doc 3000/93, June 10, 1993.

8. A Nicaraguan proposal that the membership of the IAHRC be increased to eleven is pending approval.

9. CICAD was established in 1986 but did not begin operating until 1988.

10. "Security" is used here in the narrow conventional sense of self-defense and armed forces. Although security matters could be subsumed under the "political" rubric, it is treated separately in OAS usage.

11. AG/RES 1121 (XXI-0/91), approved June 8, 1991.

12. AG/RES 1179 (XXII-0/92), approved May 23, 1992.

13. OEA/Ser. P, AG/doc 3020/93, June 11, 1993. The Special Committee has been authorized to hold a conference of "government experts on security mechanisms and measures to promote confidence in the region" before the next General Assembly.

14. The Inter-American Defense Board predates the OAS, having been established in 1942 in the middle of World War II. Although its budget is part of the OAS general budget, it functions independently of the Secretariat and the Permanent Council. Its members report directly to their defense ministries and/or services. Its chairman is always a U.S. citizen, and some governments see it as a U.S.-dominated instrument. It has in the past also had the reputation of being a convenient "exile" for officers who are in disfavor or politically controversial. The Board established and operates, largely with U.S. funds, the Inter-American Defense College, which is located on a U.S. military post (Fort McNair, in Washington, D.C.).

15. OEA/Ser. P, AG/doc 3015/93 rev 1, June 11, 1993.

16. "Exposition of the Permanent Representative of Chile in the session of the Special Committee on Reforms to the Charter, September 17, 1992." The text of this speech was published in the *Report of the Special Committee on Reforms to the Charter*, OEA/Ser. G, CP/doc 2311/92, rev l, October 15, 1992. The English translation is the author's. An excellent historical account of the development of a doctrine of democratic governance in the inter-American system is contained in Heraldo Muñoz, "The OAS and Democratic Governance," *Journal of Democracy* 4, no. 3 (July 1993): 29–38.

17. "The solidarity of the American States and the high aims which are sought through it require the political organization of those States on the basis of the effective exercise of representative democracy." Chapter II, Article 3(d) of the OAS Charter.

18. In 1973, largely to permit member states to renew relations with Cuba, the 3d General Assembly approved a resolution allowing for "ideological pluralism" (AG/RES 128 [III-073], April 15, 1973). Selectively quoting from the Charter on nonintervention, the resolution declared that every state had the right to adopt "its own system of government and economic and social organization"; it went on to proclaim that, under the Charter, "plurality of ideologies is a presupposition of regional solidarity." The sense of the resolution stands in contradiction to other parts of the Charter which declare representative democracy to be essential.

19. "Convinced that representative democracy is an indispensable condition for the stability, peace and development of the region . . ."—preamble as amended by the 1985 Protocol of Cartagena reforms. Some eight countries, including the United States, have not ratified the Protocol of Cartagena, and it is not in force for those countries.

20. Protocol of Washington, approved December 14, 1992. This protocol also covered economic reforms, as noted earlier.

21. Resolution of the 17th Meeting of Foreign Ministers, June 23, 1979.

22. "Unit for Democratic Development," AG/RES 1063 (XX-0/90), June 8, 1990; and "Program of Support for the Promotion of Democracy," CP/RES 572 (882/91), December 10, 1991.

23. OEA/Ser. P, AG/doc 3013/93, rev 1, June 9, 1993.

24. An agreement between the OAS and the government of Suriname establishing the OAS mission and specifying its functions was signed July 21, 1992. The OAS helped negotiate an "Agreement for National Reconciliation and Development" between the Suriname government and the two insurgent groups, the Jungle Command and the Tucajana Amazones, which was signed August 8, 1992.

25. MRE/RES 3/92, December 14, 1992.

26. MRE/RES 2/93, June 8, 1993.

27. The international mission is composed at present of some 130 civilian observers distributed through nine departments in Haiti, all but 20 or so being OAS contracted personnel. The chief of the small OAS human rights observer group, which has been in Haiti since September 1992, was named executive director of the international mission. For detailed information on the mission and its current status, see the OAS Secretary-General's Report to the Ad Hoc Ministers of Foreign Affairs Meeting on Haiti, MRE/doc 6/93, June 6, 1993.

28. In the UN mediation in El Salvador in 1991–92, Mexico, Spain, the United States, and Venezuela exerted separate pressure and support on behalf of the UN mediator's efforts, and were called "Friends of El Salvador." The reference to "Friends of Haiti" obviously refers to that precedent.

29. The resolution was jointly submitted by France, Venezuela, and the United States. S/25957, June 15, 1993.

30. Howard W. French, "Restoring Stability to Haiti Is Seen as the Next Big Test," *New York Times*, July 5, 1993, p. A4.

31. The OAS is not, of course, the only international organization to adopt democracy as a requirement for its members. The European Community (EC) made very clear, in its treatment of Spain and Greece, that a democratic system was a prerequisite for participation. The Conference on Security and Cooperation in Europe (CSCE) also specifies democracy as one of its basic principles and has established both an Office of Free Elections and an Office of Democratic Institutions and Human Rights. See *The Conference on Security and Cooperation in Europe: An Overview of the CSCE Process, Recent Meetings and Institutional Developments*, prepared by the staff of the Commission on Security and Cooperation in Europe, Washington, D.C., February 1992. See also Neil J. Kritz, "The CSCE in the New Era," *Journal of Democracy* 4, no. 3 (July 1993): 17–28.

32. *Report of the Special Committee on Reforms to the Charter*. An account of the events leading up to the Washington Protocol, as well as all the major statements, arguments, and discussions of the working committee designated to prepare the session, are contained in this document. An account of the debates in the working group plus interviews is contained in an unpublished paper by Fernando H. F. Botelho, "The Organization of American States Redefined," B.A. thesis, Department of Government, Cornell University, Fall 1992.

CHAPTER 4

1. More fully, the text reads: ". . . the Rio Group has consolidated its identity and role as an international interlocutor, a role they vowed to intensify." Text of the Buenos Aires Declaration issued by the presidents of the Rio Group in Buenos Aires, December 2, 1992, reported in *Foreign Broadcast Information Service*, FBIS-LAT-92–235, December 7, 1992, p. 2.

2. For the background on CECLA, see Scheman, *The Inter-American Dilemma*, p. 4.

3. Aspen Institute, *The Planetary Bargain: Proposals for a New International Economic Order to Meet Human Needs* (Princeton, N.J.: Aspen Institute Program in International Affairs, 1975).

4. A good discussion of this point is in Anthony Arend, "The United Nations and the New World Order," *Georgetown Law Journal* 81, no. 3 (March 1993): 515–16.

5. Report by the secretary-general to the 23d General Assembly, "Cooperation between the OAS and the United Nations," OEA/Ser. P, AG/doc 2930, May 6, 1993. This report is in three parts. Part I contains the presentation that the secretary-general made orally to the UN Special Committee and expanded remarks he submitted later in writing, listed as Annexes 1 and 2. The quotation is from Annex 2, pp. 20–21.

6. For the information in this paragraph I have drawn from Arend, "The United Nations and the New World Order," pp. 500–503.

7. Ad Hoc Meeting of Foreign Ministers on Haiti, MRE/RES 4/92, December 13, 1992.

8. These are described in detail in the secretary-general's report to the 23d General Assembly, "Cooperation between the OAS and the United Nations," Part II, May 17, 1993. The different parts of this document were submitted on different dates and are hence dated differently. Part II was prepared by the General Secretariat.

9. OEA/Ser. P, AG/doc 3937/93, rev 1, June 11, 1993.

10. UN secretary-general Boutros Boutros-Ghali wrote, "It is not [my] purpose. . .to set forth any formal pattern of relationship between regional organizations and the United Nations, or to call for any specific division of labor. What is clear, however, is that regional arrangements or agencies . . . possess a potential that should be utilized in serving the functions of this report . . . . Consultations between the United Nations and regional arrangements or agencies could do much to build international consensus on the nature of a problem and the measures required to address it." Boutros Boutros-Ghali, *Agenda for Peace: Preventive Diplomacy, Peacemaking and Peace-keeping*, United Nations, New York, 1992, pp. 36–37. This document is the secretary-general's response to the invitation of the Security Council "summit meeting" on January 31, 1992, to

circulate to the UN members the secretary-general's recommendations on how to improve the UN's peacemaking capacity.

11. See OEA/Ser. G, CP/doc 2334/93, January 12, 1993.

12. *Program-Budget of the Organization for the 1994–95 Biennium, 1994 Quotas and Pledges to the Voluntary Funds*, OEA/Ser. P, AG/doc 3033/93, June 11, 1993.

13. From an oral interview with Secretariat officials.

14. Boutros-Ghali, *Agenda for Peace*, p. 9.

15. In a sense, the 1989 Panama crisis might be viewed in these terms. While Latin American nations tried to resolve the crisis, they felt in the end that the operational and legal norms of the inter-American system limited what that mission could do. The United States, unwilling to be limited by abstract precepts of international law, acted unilaterally out of the conviction that the realities of the crisis were so serious it needed to be "resolved."

16. Robert Hunter, "Why Somalia? An Experiment in Redemption," *Washington Post*, December 6, 1992, p. C1. See also the collection of essays edited by Laura W. Reed and Carl Kaysen, *Emerging Norms of Justified Intervention*, Cambridge, MA: Committee on International Security Studies, American Academy of Arts and Sciences, 1993.

17. See, for example, the comment of former U.S. representative to the United Nations Thomas Pickering ". . . the end of the Cold War does not mean that we will relinquish the option to employ force unilaterally . . . . " Thomas Pickering, "Power and Purpose: Making Multilateralism Work," *Foreign Service Journal* 69, no. 7 (July 1992): 31.

18. The Washington Protocol reform allowing for suspension of a government that comes to power unconstitutionally was approved by vote when Mexico's opposition made consensus impossible.

19. See Scheman, *The Inter-American Dilemma*, Chapter 3.

20. Boutros-Ghali, *Agenda for Peace*, p. 25.

21. Secretary-General Joao Baena Soares, "Cooperation between the Organization of American States and the United Nations System," Part I, Annex 2, pp. 17–19.

22. A particularly interesting discussion of the question of a UN military force is contained in an article by Brian Urquhart, former undersecretary-general of the UN, and a large number of subsequent commentaries on the article by diplomats, academics, and government officials. The Urquhart article, "For a UN Volunteer Military Force," appeared in *The New York Review of Books*, June 10, 1993 pp. 3–4. The commentaries appeared in the two subsequent issues of the *New York Review of Books*, June 24, 1993, pp. 58–60, July 15, 1993, pp. 52–56.

23. President Bush's address to the U.S. public on his decision to send troops to Somalia. Transcript reprinted in *New York Times*, December 5, 1992.

24. Leslie Gelb, "The UN Chief's Dilemma: Must U.S. Help Mean U.S. Control?" *New York Times*, December 31, 1992, p. A25.

Chapter 5

1. "Inter-American Program of Action for Environmental Protection," OEA/Ser. P, AG/doc 2769/91, rev 2, June 8, 1991.

2. Ernst B. Haas, *When Knowledge Is Power: Three Models of Change in International Organizations* (Berkeley: University of California Press, 1989), p. 178.

3. I have borrowed the concept of a "linchpin" role for international organizations from ibid., and suggest its application to the OAS.

A New OAS for the New Times

Heraldo Muñoz

INTRODUCTION

The Organization of American States (OAS) was created in the wake of World War II, but soon afterward it was rendered impotent by the cold war. For very different reasons, both North Americans and Latin Americans arrived at the conclusion that the organization served little useful purpose and, for many years, tended to ignore it. Important weaknesses and obstacles to the process of renewal remain, not the least of which is the asymmetrical nature of an organization comprising member countries equal in juridical terms but unequal in size and power. Nowadays, however, the end of the cold war has opened new prospects for the organization.

Governments of the region have begun to reevaluate their attitudes toward the hemispheric organization. As a result, the OAS may be reemerging from a long period of stagnation and political irrelevance. The news media are showing more lively interest in the organization. For example, after the 21st General Assembly held in Santiago in 1991, the OAS was the object of almost simultaneous positive editorials in *Pravda* and in the *Washington Post*, while the *New York Times* published an important piece about the Santiago meeting in a Sunday edition.[1]

The new attitude toward the OAS could be clearly perceived from a 1992 statement by U.S. assistant secretary of state for inter-American affairs, Bernard W. Aronson. He recalled that when he first assumed the post, many issues dealing with Latin America actually obligated him to travel to Moscow, while "today when I think of how to deal with the problems of the region, I am more likely to go down the street to the O.A.S. headquarters."[2]

It is not certain, however, that the renewed governmental and media attention paid to the OAS indeed signals its revitalization and that the organization really serves important purposes in a post-cold war context in which so many assumptions, arrangements, and institutions born out of World War II have either disappeared or are no longer valid. The OAS agenda is in fact changing to reflect broader world transformations. The promotion and preservation of democracy is now the principal issue that defines the public profile of the OAS, in effect, the one that will determine its destiny. It will be judged by governments and public opinion precisely by what it does, or does not do, to safeguard political rights and freedoms. The organization's new activism on behalf of democracy is in accordance with a long-standing doctrine of democratic governance in the inter-American system.

The Organization of American States is, in essence, a *political* organization that serves as the principal hemispheric forum for dialogue and negotiation on the most relevant political issues of significance to the member states. There are, of course, other organizations that deal with economic issues such as trade, aid, and technical assistance. However, until recently, even on vital matters of interstate relations such as debt renegotiations and the Central American conflict, neither the United States nor the Latin American and Caribbean countries assigned much importance to the OAS as a forum, preferring to take action unilaterally, bilaterally, or through other international organizations. This situation has changed in the 1990s. New OAS instruments have been created to deal with breakdowns of democratic regimes as in Haiti and Peru; Suriname's warring factions were guided through the process of internal disarmament and reconciliation; OAS electoral observation is requested regularly by governments of the region; new member states have joined; and issues like the "Enterprise for the Americas Initiative" have been brought forward and discussed in the organization. Democracy in the Americas, though, will continue to be at the forefront of OAS concerns in the years to come, determining its future as a regional organization in the post-cold war era.

CHAPTER 1

THE OAS AND THE PROMOTION OF DEMOCRACY

With the end of the cold war has come a worldwide validation of free elections, democratic politics, and open markets.[1] This is evident from South Africa to Poland, and from the final collapse and disappearance of the Soviet Union to the growing demands for democracy in various African and Asian countries. The appeal of centrally planned economies is gone, and the very notion of dictatorship (either of the right or of the left) has become highly suspect.

Latin America has hardly been isolated from this global tendency. For the first time in decades, freely elected governments prevail throughout the region. The OAS made a historic stride in the affirmation and defense of democracy when the ministers of foreign affairs of the Americas in June 1991 signed the "Santiago Commitment to Democracy and the Renewal of the Inter-American System,"[2] which created a mechanism for an automatic response to any illegal interruption of the democratic process in any country in the hemisphere (see Appendixes 1 and 2). In the cases of Haiti, Peru, and Guatemala, this allowed the organization to act promptly. Such a provision was seen as necessary because serious threats of intolerance, lingering authoritarian inclinations, and economic and social inequities still hover over democratic regimes.

While the Santiago Commitment and its accompanying resolution on representative democracy are both milestones in the effective safeguarding of democracy in the Americas, they are only the most recent expression of time-honored principles. The exercise of representative democracy is a cornerstone of the OAS Charter, and this is reflected, more importantly, in a multitude of declarations, resolutions, and actions taken by the organization throughout several decades. In the Americas, democracy and human rights protection have developed well beyond what other regions have achieved in terms of a moral, political, and juridical obligation. No other regional or global organization, including the United Nations, has in its charter the principle of promoting representative democracy as a basic goal.

It should be noted, however, that often practice has not matched the high-minded declarations of support for democracy in the inter-American system. The doctrine on democratic governance many times was not implemented because power politics intervened. The national interest of the United States, and in some cases the national interests of Latin American countries, dictated outcomes contrary to the spirit of the Charter. In fact, throughout the evolution of the inter-American system, whenever U.S. security and economic interests clashed with democracy promotion, the latter ideal was downplayed or ignored. Although there were some exceptions, "realpolitik" criteria like fighting communism or maintaining political stability generally triumphed, particularly during the height of the cold war. The inter-American commitment to democracy has never rested solely on doctrine. Until recent times, however, words were more abundant than deeds.

THE EMERGENCE OF A DOCTRINE OF DEMOCRATIC GOVERNANCE IN THE INTER-AMERICAN SYSTEM

Democratic government has been a goal of the peoples of the Americas almost since the time of their independence and the collapse of the power that absolute monarchies held over them. By the year 1826, there was already talk in Latin America of republican as opposed to monarchist states.

The Washington Conference of 1907 formalized the principle of democratic governance in the Central American region. In the General Treaty of Peace and Friendship that issued from the conference, the republics of the isthmus agreed, among other points, not to recognize Central American governments that emerged from rebellions rather than free elections. At another conference in 1922–23, the Central American countries reaffirmed the 1907 agreements and went further to prohibit the recognition of governments installed by force, even if consecrated later by free elections. The United States in the early part of the century had an activist policy of fostering democracy in the region, particularly in Central America and the Caribbean, lasting until the Hoover administration.[3] Apparently, the Great Depression stemmed the democracy drive in the Americas, shifting U.S. emphasis and attention to domestic economic issues.

In the context of the inter-American system, the first official recognition of the "existence of democracy as a common cause in America" is found in the Declaration of Principles on Inter-American Solidarity and Cooperation of the Inter-American Conference on the Consolidation of Peace held in Buenos Aires in 1936. From 1936 to 1945, each succeeding inter-American conference reiterated that declaration in connection with some aspect of its work.

On November 21, 1945, the Uruguayan minister of foreign affairs, Dr. Eduardo Rodríguez Larreta, addressed a note to the other American governments in which he proposed multilateral action to defend democracy and human rights. His proposal—enthusiastically endorsed by U.S. secretary of state James F. Byrnes—underscored the parallel that existed between the defense of human liberty and maintaining the peace. But the action he called for stopped short of violating the principle of nonintervention. Though the proposal was not approved, it was indicative of continuing hemispheric concern over the defense of democracy.

The Inter-American Conference on Problems of War and Peace, held in Mexico City in 1945, produced a document known as the Declaration of Mexico, which maintained as an essential principle of the hemispheric community that "American man cannot conceive of living without justice," nor can he conceive of "living without liberty." Another resolution, entitled "The Preservation and Defense of Democracy in America," instructed the Inter-American Juridical Committee to consider a draft report submitted by Guatemala in opposition to the future installation of antidemocratic regimes in the region and to present it at the Ninth American International Conference. The Ninth Conference, the historic Conference of Bogotá held in 1948, adopted a resolution in which the American states reaffirmed "their conviction that only under a system founded upon a guarantee of the essential freedoms and rights of the individual" can the goal of effective social and economic development be attained. It furthermore condemned "the methods of every system tending to suppress political and civil rights and liberties. . . ."[4] These same principles had already been included in the preamble of the 1947 Inter-American Reciprocal Assistance Treaty (TIAR).

The Conference of Bogotá marked the genesis of the Organization of American States. It ended with the signature of the OAS Charter and the American Declaration of the Rights and Duties of Man. As former president of Colombia Alberto Lleras said in referring to the principles of the Charter, once entered into force such principles became "norms of an unquestionably binding nature, even though they had always had unequivocal moral force in the resolutions and declarations that preceded the Charter." The Charter is quite clear. Its preamble states that "the true significance of American solidarity and good neighborliness can only mean the consolidation on this continent, within the framework of democratic institutions, of a system of individual liberty and social justice based on respect for the essential rights of man" and later maintains that "the solidarity of the American states and the high aims which are sought through it *require* the political organization of those states on the basis of the effective exercise of representative democracy" (emphasis by author).

Needless to say, once democratic principles acquired a conventional character upon the signature and ratification of the Charter, any coups or unlawful interruption of democratic processes would indeed undermine the solidarity of the hemispheric countries and pose an obvious challenge to the underlying purpose of the Organization of American States. It could be argued further that the presence in the OAS of states ruled by nondemocratic governments is incompatible with American solidarity, as that presence impedes the organization from realizing its goals.

Interestingly enough, at the Conference of Bogotá, Brazil proposed that entry into the OAS be contingent both on a prospective member state's ratification of the Charter and on the adoption of a democratic form of government and guarantee of the fundamental rights of man. That same year, during discussions that resulted in the OAS Charter, Peru proposed that whenever a de facto government emerges, "the governments exchange views on whether or not there is a need for recognition and the timing of when this should be done. . . ."

After the Conference of Bogotá, a resurgence of dictatorial governments in Latin America slowed down the development of additional inter-American initiatives in furtherance of representative democracy. Between late 1948 and mid-1954, half a dozen democratic regimes were overthrown and replaced by military dictatorships. Efforts aimed at reversing the trend, including the famous "Caribbean Legion" of exiled leaders that, during 1947–49, attempted to launch collective actions in support of democracy in the Caribbean and Central America, did not prosper.[5] Nevertheless, several meetings and inter-American conferences reaffirmed, at least in theory, the hemispheric commitment to representative democracy and democratic solidarity in the Americas.

A decade beyond Bogotá, the fifth Meeting of Consultation of Ministers of Foreign Affairs, held in Santiago in August 1959, marked a major milestone in the development of the inter-American doctrine of democratic governance. From the meeting emerged a partial list of the attributes of a representative democracy. The Inter-American Juridical Committee was asked to draft a convention on human rights that would consider the legal relationship between respect for human rights and the effective exercise of representative democracy. The Committee was also asked to come up with a draft convention on the effective exercise of representative democracy. Moreover, the fifth Meeting of Consultation unequivocally stated in the Declaration of Santiago that

> the existence of anti-democratic regimes constitutes a violation of the principles on which the Organization of American States is founded, and a danger to united and peaceful relationships in the hemisphere.

The report of the inter-American Juridical Committee reaffirmed the interrelationship between human rights and exercise of democracy and upheld the binding nature of the principles of the Charter, but in its report approved by the majority, collective action in defense of or on behalf of the restoration of democracy was seen as inadmissible under the terms of the Charter of Bogotá. The draft convention on the effective exercise of representative democracy was judged too controversial and was not endorsed by the member states.

From 1959 on, there was intensive activity to clarify the scope of the hemisphere's democratic commitment. Despite the cold war, the impact of the Cuban revolution, and the prevalence of dictatorial regimes during the 1960s and 1970s, several inter-American meetings continued to reaffirm the concepts of liberty and representative democracy set forth in the Charter and to issue relevant proposals.

Perhaps one of the earliest but least-known indications that the OAS member states were concerned over the merit and limits of involving the organization in specific steps to preserve democracy and safeguard against coups d'etat happened in August 1962. At that time, several special meetings of the Permanent Council were held to consider a request by the governments of the Dominican Republic, Venezuela, Honduras, and Costa Rica that a Meeting of Consultation of Ministers of Foreign Affairs be called to "reaffirm democratic solidarity in America and to consider what attitude the governments of the member States should adopt vis-a-vis coup d'etat regimes." The request, fed by anxiety over a coup in Peru, stimulated a substantive debate and subsequently a vote, which fell short of the necessary majority. Interestingly, the United States adopted a cautious stand and did not join the effort to request a Meeting of Consultation. Apparently, Washington's vote of abstention reflected a desire not to disturb the existing coalition of anti-Communist governments in the region. The numerous dictatorial governments in the region, as well as the sharpening of the East-West conflict, frustrated that early attempt to discuss specific ways to implement the principle of democratic solidarity in the Americas.

In November 1963, the OAS Permanent Council adopted a resolution calling for a Meeting of Consultation of Foreign Ministers on representative democracy. Given the urgency and importance of the topics to be dealt with, it was eventually decided that they should be examined at an inter-American conference rather than a foreign ministers' meeting. The Second Special Inter-American Conference, held in Rio de Janeiro in November 1965, adopted an interesting resolution entitled "Informal Procedure on Recognition of de facto Governments," in which it was recommended that the member states, immediately after the overthrow of a legitimate government, initiate exchanges with one another on the situation. Bearing in mind the willingness of the de facto government to hold free elections within a reasonable period and its commitment to meet other international obligations, once consultations have taken place "each government shall decide whether to maintain diplomatic relations with the de facto government." Despite its substantive weakness, the resolution reflected the continuing impulse to confront antidemocratic regimes on a multilateral footing.

During the 1980s, with the return to democracy in most Latin American nations, the issue of effective representative government again became a focal point of dialogue in the inter-American system. Thus the 1984 OAS General Assembly, meeting in Brasilia, expressed the willingness of the member states to join efforts to ensure the peoples of the Americas a life of "freedom and dignity." The same assembly convened a special session, to be held in 1985, for the purpose of examining and, if appropriate, adopting draft amendments to the Charter of the OAS.

The Special General Assembly, held in Cartagena, Colombia, in 1985, approved another milestone, a protocol of amendment to the OAS Charter. On that occasion, the following phrase was added to the preamble of the Charter: "Representative democracy is an indispensable condition for the stability, peace and development of the region." Still more important, to the essential purposes of the organization described in Chapter I was added: "To promote and consolidate representative democracy, with due respect for the principle of non-intervention."

The gradual return to democracy in Latin American countries gave form to the democratic ideals of the OAS Charter. A resolution of the

General Assembly, meeting in Guatemala in 1986, declared that "for the first time in many decades, many member States held free elections, with the result that democratic, representative and pluralist systems of government have been established, and it is the aim of the Organization of American States to promote and consolidate representative democracy while respecting the principle of non-intervention." It urged "the governments of the Americas whose societies have problems that call for reconciliation and national unity to undertake or continue a genuine dialogue" decisively conducive to "improving the human rights situation and to strengthening the representative and pluralist democratic system."[6]

The new democracy-related contractual aspects of the Charter as amended at Cartagena, which entered into force in November 1988, were reaffirmed in the Declaration of Asunción, signed at the General Assembly held in Paraguay in June 1990. They were developed for the first time in operative form in the Santiago Commitment and in its companion resolution on representative democracy.

From Doctrine to Uneven Practice:
OAS Actions in the Name of Representative Democracy

Efforts to restore democracy in Haiti, Peru, and Guatemala as well as the recent contributions made by the OAS in the observation of electoral processes in Nicaragua, El Salvador, Haiti, Suriname, Paraguay, and elsewhere indicate that the organization is now energetically promoting and defending representative democracy. In fact, the OAS has acquired new political relevance primarily to the extent that it has been perceived as an instrument of action on behalf of democracy.

Measures taken by the OAS in the name of democracy have a long, though irregular or inconsistent, history. For example, in the name of democracy, the OAS Permanent Council, meeting as an organ of consultation under the Rio Pact, decided in July 1960 to break diplomatic relations with the Dominican Republic and to partially cut the economic ties of the member states with that nation. Leonidas Trujillo, the Dominican Republic's strongman, had become an adversary of democracy in the Caribbean Basin, to the point of promoting subversive acts in an attempt to overthrow the Venezuelan government and its president. In part as a result of such sanctions, the OAS helped weaken the authoritarian government in the Dominican Republic, which toppled in late May 1961.

In the case of Cuba—at the height of the cold war—a meeting of foreign ministers in July 1964, acting within the framework of the Rio

Pact, condemned the Communist regime of Fidel Castro for attempting to overthrow the democratic government of Venezuela and called for the suspension of diplomatic relations as well as economic and transportation ties. Two years earlier in Punta del Este, Uruguay, again under the umbrella of the Rio Pact, the OAS by majority vote, recalling the principle of representative democracy and the Declaration of Santiago on free elections as the cornerstone of American governments, had expelled Cuba from the inter-American system, specifically noting that the Marxist-Leninist Cuban government was "incompatible with the principles and objectives of the inter-American system." Though other Latin American states were far from being free, none received this kind of treatment. The cold war was giving an East-West twist to the promotion of the democracy ideal.

In May 1965, a political crisis in the Dominican Republic shook the inter-American system. The United States, fearing a left-wing takeover, sent troops into the country. Another meeting of foreign ministers—this time outside the scope of the Rio Pact—resolved to turn the unilateral armed action of the United States into a collective operation by converting the foreign military forces on Dominican territory into an "inter-American force." One of the purposes of this move was "in a spirit of democratic impartiality, to cooperate in the restoration of normal conditions in the Dominican Republic" and in the establishment in that country of an atmosphere conducive to the "functioning of democratic institutions." However history may judge these events, it should be highlighted that within a few months, under the auspices of the inter-American force present in the Dominican Republic, elections were held that led to the reestablishment of a civilian government.

It was not until many years later that the OAS would again take action in a situation involving the issue of democratic governance. The OAS kept silent and remained on the sidelines when dictatorships in the region were at their peak from the mid-1960s to the late 1970s, convincing many people that the organization was incapable of throwing weight behind its commitment in principle to democratic solidarity in the Americas. An internal crisis in Nicaragua that intensified in the late 1970s, particularly the violation of human rights by the government of Anastasio Somoza, mobilized the inter-American system, and another meeting of foreign ministers was convened in September 1978. Although border problems between Nicaragua and Costa Rica were also involved, the meeting focused primarily on international concerns over human rights and democracy in Nicaragua. As a result, a commission on friendly cooperation and conciliation was formed and conducted talks with the Somoza government in search of a solution to the crisis. In a resolution that laid the groundwork for a definitive settlement to the conflict, the ministers declared in June 1979 that the solution in Nicaragua should be based on:

1.   Immediate and definitive replacement of the Somoza regime.

2.   Installation in Nicaragua of a democratic government, the composition of which should include the principal representative groups that oppose the Somoza regime, that reflects the free will of the people of Nicaragua.

3.   Guarantee of respect for the human rights of all Nicaraguans without exception.

4.   The holding of free elections as soon as possible, which will lead to the establishment of a truly democratic government that guarantees peace, freedom, and justice.

The clear pronouncement of the OAS, in addition to endowing the concept of nonintervention with—to say the least—a flexible meaning, reinforced the collective negotiating approach of Central American countries in favor of democracy and peace in the area. Their principal declaration took shape as the Esquipulas Accord, a major political and legal precedent establishing a linkage between peace and security in the Central American subregion and the exercise of democracy and respect for human rights within each country there. The firm OAS stand on Nicaragua occurred in a context of reaffirmation of independent foreign policy behavior on the part of many Latin American countries, in a climate of East-West détente, and at a moment when human rights became a centerpiece of U.S. foreign policy under the Carter administration while the Somoza regime's contempt for basic freedoms invited widespread international rejection. The United States, as well as many other countries, had arrived at the conclusion that an alternative—preferably moderate—had to be found to the Somoza dictatorship.

In contrast to Nicaragua, OAS action in Panama in 1989 sought a consensus formula with General Manuel Antonio Noriega that would respect the sovereign will of the Panamanian people expressed in free elections. Nothing came of this initiative. Independently of other external reasons for its failure, the Panama demarche revealed the inadequacy of OAS procedures for implementing the principles of representative democracy set forth in the Charter. The General Assembly meeting in Santiago remedied this inadequacy fairly well when it adopted the Santiago Commitment and the mechanism set out in the counterpart resolution on the defense of representative democracy. Their significance, according to one author, is that they constitute a major step toward the validation of democratic politics and the emergence of a "right to democratic governance."[7]

The most recent step in the development of an inter-American doctrine of democratic governance was the reform of the OAS Charter—the so-called Washington protocol—approved in December 1992 that, once ratified, will allow for the suspension from the organization of member states in which a democratically elected government is overthrown through the use of force. This important reform, originally proposed by Argentina, was also accompanied by Charter modifications underlining the organization's resolve to confront poverty as a major roadblock to consolidation of democratic rule.[8]

THE OAS AND DEMOCRACY:
RECENT ACTIONS AND SOME SUGGESTIONS

In recent years, the OAS has taken important steps toward codifying the abundant precedents for further hemispheric action on behalf of democracy. Why did OAS countries at this point in time decide to authorize such important initiatives as the Santiago Commitment and the associated resolution for the protection of representative democracy? Surely, it had something to do with the end of the cold war. The passing of that conflict sharply reduced the risk that resolutions endorsing hemispheric action on behalf of democracy would be treated as licenses for the pursuit of unrelated political ends. Additionally, there was in this period—particularly among Latin American countries—a shared desire to safeguard and consolidate the newly regained democratic freedoms after a long period of dictatorial rule.

When on September 30, 1991, the military forces of Haiti ousted President Jean-Bertrand Aristide, they triggered the mechanism created in Santiago. Within a few days, the foreign ministers assembled in Washington and resolved to recognize President Aristide and his appointees as Haiti's only legitimate government and to recommend that all OAS member states take specific steps to isolate economically and diplomatically the group that had seized control. In addition, they dispatched to Haiti a special mission composed of foreign ministers and the secretary-general with a mandate to press for the restoration of the democratically elected government.

When that mission failed to achieve its objective, the ministers reconvened and stiffened their recommendations to include the immediate freezing of all assets of the Haitian state held in any OAS member country. In addition, they outlined cooperation plans to be implemented once President Aristide's administration was restored and explored means for strengthening constitutional democracy in Haiti.

In May 1992, the OAS foreign ministers went further to recommend to member states, among other measures, the denial of access to port facilities to any vessels that violated the embargo, OAS monitoring of compliance with the embargo, and the denial of visas to "perpetrators and supporters of the coup" in Haiti. When it became apparent that the trade embargo was clearly failing, due in large part to violations by nonhemispheric countries, the foreign ministers urged all members of the OAS as well as the United Nations that had not done so to fully implement the measures agreed upon by the ad hoc meetings of foreign ministers. Pressure mounted to involve the United Nations actively. In December 1992, a resolution passed by the foreign ministers of the hemisphere mandated the secretary-general of the OAS "to explore the possibility and convenience" of taking the Haitian situation to the UN Security Council to obtain the desired universal application of the trade embargo. The designation by the UN secretary-general of Dante Caputo, former minister of foreign affairs of Argentina, as special envoy for Haiti and Caputo's simultaneous nomination as representative of the OAS secretary-general placed the Haiti affair in a new phase of cooperation between the two organizations in continuing to ratchet up pressure on the de facto regime.

Finally, because the trade embargo had not been adhered to by countries outside the hemisphere and because negotiations for a political solution to the Haitian crisis continued to be blocked by the de facto authorities, the legitimate Aristide government formally requested, in June 1993, the intervention of the Security Council of the United Nations. In a landmark resolution (no. 841), the Security Council decided to impose a worldwide oil embargo and banned arms shipments to Haiti. It also froze the assets abroad controlled by the military government of Haiti.

Despite the reference in Resolution 841 to a "unique and exceptional situation" in Haiti, and the statement made by the president of the Security Council that the resolution in question did not constitute a precedent, the fact is that it was the first time that an internal political crisis having to do with democratic governance provoked such drastic measures on the part of the UN. This resolution can be interpreted as a further step in the collective action in defense of democracy, this time extending beyond the Western Hemisphere (but in support of measures adopted by the foreign ministers of the Americas within the OAS framework).

Up to this point, and despite an important agreement reached directly by the Haitians in July 1993, under UN and OAS auspices, the OAS-UN efforts have not yet dislodged the de facto government. The lack of real progress has been linked by some critics to Haiti's long history of undemocratic rule. Nevertheless, seen against the hemisphere's traditional pattern of acquiescence, however grudging, in military coups d'etat, the Haitian case at least has signaled the crystallization in the Americas of a firm will to resist the enemies of democratic government.

The Santiago mechanism was activated a second time when, on April 5, 1992, democratically elected President Alberto Fujimori of Peru illegally closed Congress, froze out the judiciary, arrested several congressmen and political and labor union leaders, and suspended freedom of expression and other civic rights. A few days later, the OAS foreign ministers met and "deeply deplored" President Fujimori's actions, urged the restoration of democratic rule, and called on the Peruvian authorities to fully respect human rights. At the same time, the ministers appointed a special diplomatic mission to travel to Peru to promote negotiations between the government and opposition forces for the reestablishment of full democracy.

Some countries, including the United States, cut economic aid to Peru, while the Rio Group suspended Peru from attending its meetings. At the OAS meeting of foreign ministers on Peru held in Nassau, Bahamas, in May 1992, President Fujimori made an unexpected appearance and, reversing earlier statements, committed himself to democratic restoration in his country through a process culminating in the election of a democratic constitutional congress.

The elections to the constitutional body took place in late November 1992 with the participation of some opposition forces while others abstained, alleging lack of sufficient guarantees for free and fair elections, and with electoral observation provided by the Organization of American States. Sometime later, municipal elections were held, also with the electoral supervision of the OAS. Clearly, the elections represented a step in the right direction but by no means ensured the full return to democratic rule in Peru.

When on May 25, 1993, the president of Guatemala, Jorge Serrano, suspended constitutional guarantees in what amounted to a self-inflicted coup d'etat, the hemispheric community reacted quickly and forcefully under the mechanism created in Santiago through Resolution 1080. That same day, the Permanent Council called for an emergency meeting of foreign ministers, while the secretary-general of the OAS, Joao Baena Soares, accompanied by three Central American foreign ministers, traveled to Guatemala on a fact-finding mission. They warned President Serrano and the Guatemalan armed forces of the eventual international consequences of the actions taken against democracy.

By the time the foreign ministers assembled in Washington on June 3, Serrano had left office. When the OAS ministers gathered once again to consider the Guatemala situation on June 6, following another visit to the Central American nation by the secretary-general, constitutional democracy had returned to Guatemala, and the former attorney general for human rights, Ramiro de León Carpio, had been designated by its Congress as the new president. The OAS, according to the new president, had played a critical role in support of the domestic efforts to regain democracy in Guatemala.

Beyond the success in the Guatemala case, the meager results of the organization's actions toward Haiti and Peru suggest that the OAS may need to adopt additional instruments and measures for the defense of democracy.[9] On the contrary, it may be argued that legal theory does not demand them, and that what is required is an addition not of language but of will. However, that would be an oversimplification. Will must be exerted if it is to have the desired deterrent effect. The Santiago resolution does not enumerate the sanctions that the organization is prepared to employ against an illegitimate regime, although the resolutions on Haiti approved by the ad hoc meetings of foreign ministers list a whole range of steps recommended to discomfit the Haitian dictatorship. Systematizing such measures for future cases may now be needed. The very act of compiling a list of penalties in conjunction with operational plans for implementing them stiffens the commitment of member states, transmits a warning message, and, if deterrence fails, allows for unified, cogent action on the part of member states.

Is a consensus for the threat or the use of force as a last resort likely to form in any imaginable case? The collective response to the overthrow of democracy in Haiti offers grounds for doubt. Economic sanctions—particularly the trade embargo—have not been adhered to by countries outside the hemisphere. Moreover, they have apparently hurt the average citizen without threatening the putschists' control. To be sure, the mixed outcome of economic sanctions in the Haitian case does not guarantee that they would be ineffective in other cases. In some cases, it may be more efficacious to target the economic resources of delinquent individuals like the domestic financiers of the Haitian soldiers' coup. Targeting requires knowledge, or the means to rapidly acquire knowledge, about the location of the offenders' assets. Sanctions probably work least well when directed against economies in which subsistence agriculture predominates. Countries with large urban populations and a substantial middle class will generally prove more vulnerable. Nevertheless, as the case of Panama demonstrates, a military government may be able to sustain control even in the face of sanctions that inflict widespread damage upon the civilian population.

Force as a means of ousting a regime will probably continue to be unacceptable to a substantial number of hemispheric governments and nongovernmental entities. The problem of who will exercise and control the use of force in an asymmetrical hemispheric context is one reason why. The peril of selective application due to power-politics motivations is clearly another.

That the member states should feel great reluctance about employing arms for the defense of democracy is not without base. Leaving aside important questions of international law,[10] even when it achieves its immediate objective, military action can result in serious collateral harm to innocent people and their property. Moreover, if democratic institutions were not deeply rooted in a country where force has been applied, their reconsolidation may require time and protection. Thus, if collective action were to achieve its broader goal, the organization might have to sustain its presence beyond the campaign to displace an illegal regime. The cost and complications of open-ended involvement are very real disincentives to direct action against antidemocratic governments.

No consensus exists within the OAS for military action against a dictatorial government. There is probably not a consensus for armed peacemaking to assist in the restoration of democracy either. Yet the smaller members in the Caribbean in particular are concerned by the prospect of power being seized by a handful of thugs who may be surreptitiously armed, trained, and influenced by foreign elements, not necessarily governmental ones. One way of reconciling doubts among some members about OAS-authorized military actions with the legitimate concerns of others may be a pact among states willing to use force to assist each other in guaranteeing the survival of democracy. Of course, the more states that participate in such pacts, the less the danger of intervention for ulterior motives.

A more solid foundation is present in hemispheric politics for peaceful collective action in favor of democracy and to deter coups d'etat, provided by the important OAS Charter reform, approved in December 1992, that introduced the temporary suspension of member states whose democratic governance is forcibly interrupted.[11] Identifying and implementing an appropriate response to the overthrow of a democratically elected government (or the imminent threat thereof) is difficult and demanding work. At this point the OAS has no choice but to improvise a response. That will not do. The mission is far too complex and demanding.

One complexity stems from the fact that threats to democratic government do not always originate in the cantonments of the armed forces. It follows that the organization requires a cadre of professionals from which it can draw for fact-finding at any time.

The newly established "Unit for Democracy Promotion" within the OAS might assume such responsibility. The unit, created by a decision of the 1990 General Assembly, could add to the tasks already identified, such as providing governments with technical assistance on election monitoring and facilitating the exchange of ideas and experiences about the strengthening of democratic institutions. As a further step toward implementing the Santiago Commitment, the OAS member states could elevate the unit to under-Secretariat level and provide it with material resources proportional to the magnitude of its tasks. The same kind of support is needed for the Inter-American Commission on Human Rights, an OAS organ that continues to play an important role in the defense of liberty and human dignity.

A serious commitment to strengthening democracy must encompass economic policy as well. The OAS can play a role in economic reform and development, but most of its efforts will have to be carried out in conjunction with more specialized institutions like the Inter-American Development Bank or the regional agencies of the United Nations. Prominent among the issues discussed in OAS forums in recent years is the alleviation of Latin America's debilitating debt burden. Although no longer as dramatic an issue in the region as in the 1980s, the enormity of the debt (in excess of $420 billion), coupled with interest payments of roughly $35 billion a year, has crippled economic growth in many countries and forced the adoption of austerity measures that have downgraded long-term potential for growth, dragged millions into extreme poverty, and associated democratic governments in the popular mind with deprivation, thus inhibiting their efforts to deepen democracy through the transformation of rigid and grossly inequitable social and economic structures.

The OAS could provide the leadership to alleviate this crushing burden and its harmful aftereffects. In the name of consolidating democracy, an OECD-led coalition of countries orchestrated a 50 percent cut in Poland's foreign debt. That debt-reduction rationale is equally applicable to the countries of Latin America, which could benefit from a "Debt for Democracy" scheme that goes beyond existing programs. Such schemes could even countenance the purchase of small amounts of privately owed debt in exchange for setting up democracy promotion projects in the pertinent countries.

Democracies in Latin America and the Caribbean also confront the reluctance of the great industrial states to match their high-flown rhetoric about the uninhibited play of market forces with practice. Under extraordinarily difficult circumstances, Latin American states have reduced the size of their public sector, slashed economic regulations, and generally oriented themselves toward full participation in the global economy. Protectionism by the industrial North mocks their efforts to compete and threatens their economic and political stability.

In the launching of the North American free trade negotiations and the Enterprise for the Americas Initiative, the first steps were taken toward the establishment of a hemisphere-wide free trade community. Economic integration offers an unprecedented opportunity to cement the bonds of representative government in the Americas. As the European Community expanded from its original core, it used democracy as a fundamental criterion for membership, refusing Spain, Portugal, and Greece consideration until they became democratic states. Likewise, in 1986 when Argentina and Brazil signed a far-reaching economic agreement that gave birth to the MERCOSUR free trade zone, they stressed that an important purpose was "to consolidate democracy as a way of life and a system of government." Their presidents declared that a "basic requirement" for the participation of third parties was that they be democratic countries. As the North American Free Trade Zone expands southward, it can set similar standards. Both governmental leaders and nongovernmental organizations throughout the hemisphere could identify criteria that might stimulate and consolidate democratic practice as economic integration proceeds.

Still, although there is indeed a vital role for the international community in fostering and safeguarding democratic governance, it must be kept in mind that democracy in any country ultimately rests in the hands of its people and depends on the existence of a civil society that can effectively use the governing instruments at its disposal.

CHAPTER 2

THE REEMERGENCE OF MULTILATERALISM

THE CHANGING HEMISPHERIC AGENDA

Democracy is the centerpiece of the emerging "new" OAS. However, the hemispheric agenda of the 1990s goes beyond the question of democratic governance, as can be seen by examining the new committees, programs, and activities of the organization. The sea changes in the international environment have posed opportunities for the renewal of the OAS as well as underlined some of its enduring limitations. For instance, there is the relative decline of the old military-strategic component of regional security. A working group on hemispheric security, created at the 1991 General Assembly,[1] has begun rethinking hemispheric security and specifically the role of the Inter-American Defense Board (IADB) and its Inter-American Defense College, redefining their connections to the OAS. There is a strong argument for bringing both under the civilian-diplomatic control of the OAS, to confine the IADB's scope of action to technical assistance on specific military or security-related matters (for example, the IADB is undertaking, at the request of the OAS, a project to remove thousands of land mines along the Nicaragua-Honduras border left behind from the armed conflicts that ravaged the Central American isthmus during the 1980s), while serving as a meeting ground for civilian and military officials from the Americas. Following this logic, the IADB has opened its membership to all member countries of the OAS, not merely to the signatories of the Rio Pact.

In recent years, the OAS has been involved in activities that fall somewhere between security, unarmed peacekeeping, and democracy-building. Since its creation in 1990, the International Commission of

Support and Verification (CIAV-OAS) has been overseeing the disarmament and social reintegration of the ex-contras in Nicaragua. Along with observation of the 1990 Nicaraguan elections, this task was requested of the OAS under the terms of the peace agreement of Tela, Honduras, in August 1989. The CIAV-OAS not only has been involved in disarming, feeding, and protecting the former contras as they returned to Nicaragua from camps in Honduras, but also in developing a self-help housing program and in extending humanitarian services to ex-Sandinista fighters. The CIAV-OAS demobilization effort has covered about 30,000 contras. Most importantly, the CIAV-OAS international staff in Nicaragua, which by early 1993 was down to 23 people, has played a key mediation role between the armed opposition and the Nicaraguan government.[2]

The OAS has carried out similar tasks in the case of Suriname. At the invitation of the Surinamese government, the organization became involved in formalizing and safeguarding a durable peace in the interior of the country. The government also allowed the OAS to collaborate in the promotion and strengthening of democracy. Peace negotiations between the government and rebel groups culminated successfully in August 1992, and the demobilization process ensued. An OAS mission witnessed the destruction of weapons and other military hardware. By 1993, the OAS role in Suriname had shifted to development assistance, civic education, and similar activities in support of democratic institutions.[3]

While the OAS has a long history of technical cooperation on matters related to natural resources and environmental management, only in 1991 did it take up the matter of environmental well-being—viewed by some as a new "security" issue—at the political level. An inter-American program of action for environmental protection was approved, creating a Permanent Committee on the Environment within the Permanent Council, and various activities were initiated—ranging from publications to seminars and training workshops—to comply with measures recommended in the inter-American program of action.[4]

A document entitled *The Organization of American States and the Issues of Environment and Development*,[5] prepared for the Conference on the Environment and Development held in Rio de Janeiro in June 1992, summarized the main priorities of the OAS regarding the environment: the need to harmonize the expansion of international trade with environmental protection, the imperative of rethinking economic theory to take into account the environment, environmental law, technological cooperation for sustainable development, and improving public education and public awareness of the challenge of environmental protection in the Americas.

The international economy has changed radically in recent years. Globalization of economic affairs has increased interdependence enormously. The new technological revolution has brought into question the notion of "national" economies and has altered the very nature of production, with inputs of knowledge becoming more important than capital, labor, and natural resources. Yet the arguments of politically powerful groups in favor of "managed" or regulated trade instead of free trade and the formation of regional trade blocs has led some to believe that trade wars could replace the cold war.

Despite the host of institutions—public and private—involved in managing the international economy, the OAS has been playing recently a useful, if limited, role in this area. In 1991, it created a working group of the Permanent Council on the Enterprise for the Americas Initiative, which monitors the tendency toward free trade in the Americas and functions as a clearinghouse for up-to-date information on trade matters.[6] More importantly, a process of reform has begun to revamp thoroughly the old OAS Special Commission on Consultation and Negotiation (CECON), which during the 1960s and 1970s was a forum of confrontation on economic issues between, on one side, Latin America and the Caribbean and, on the other, the United States. Eventually, this led to inactivity and political irrelevance for CECON. OAS plans now contemplate its transformation into a high-level hemispheric Commission on Trade.

The OAS and its predecessors have had a long history of dealing with the narcotics trafficking problem. But beginning in the mid-1980s, as the problem intensified, the organization introduced new programs and initiatives. In 1986, the Inter-American Drug Abuse Control Commission (CICAD) was established to develop, coordinate, evaluate, and monitor the Program of Action of Rio de Janeiro against the Illicit Use, Production and Trafficking of Narcotic Drugs and Psychotropic Substances. CICAD's main objective consists of the elimination of illicit drug trafficking and drug abuse in the inter-American region through hemispheric cooperation. One interesting feature of the commission is that it has an executive secretariat with considerable autonomy.

While CICAD is not an enforcement agency, it has defined five main areas of action: legal development, education for prevention of drug abuse, community mobilization, harmonization of statistical systems, and access to information. CICAD has helped member states standardize national laws, regulations, and procedures for dealing with the interlocking chain of illicit trafficking activities and facilitated application of the 1988 U.S. Convention against Illicit Traffic in Narcotic Drugs and Psychotropic Substances throughout the region. CICAD also prepared and later approved a set of model regulations to control chemical precursors and chemical substances, machines, and materials. Twelve countries have already incorporated into legislation principles contained in these regulations. Early in 1992, a group of experts from CICAD developed a set of model regulations for procedures on the seizure of assets derived from illicit drug trafficking and money laundering.

The purpose of public health education is to complement legal, moral, and societal constraints against drug use by incorporating drug prevention programs into schools throughout the hemisphere. CICAD has organized different seminars in several countries and has worked with the Inter-American Development Bank as well as with other public and private agencies to obtain financial support for educational programs.

CICAD began activities in the area of community mobilization in early 1989. It has organized various workshops involving the private sector in the member states, the media, corporations, and voluntary organizations in the struggle against drug abuse through education and public awareness of the problem.

An inter-American data bank, financed by Japan, is now functioning. The database has been expanded; working relationships have been established with drug data collection agencies in various member states, and CICAD continues to develop common definitions and procedures for collecting, storing, and publishing data. Seminars for technical personnel have been presented in several countries. CICAD has improved information access by helping to organize an Inter-American Drug Information System (IADIS), which is presently developing a specialized collection of audiovisual materials and publications to help in the prevention of drug abuse in the Americas.

Despite the growing reputation of CICAD as a professionally competent and fully committed OAS organ, it has yet to be awarded a central role in the hemispheric campaign against the illicit trade in narcotics. One reason may be the continuing tendency of the United States to fight drugs on the basis of bilateral agreements with various countries of the region.[7]

HOW MULTILATERAL IS THE OAS?

Most of the critical issues of the post-cold war era—democracy promotion, free trade, drug trafficking—are regional in nature and cannot be addressed successfully except through cooperative, hemisphere-wide efforts. The OAS is therefore seen by many countries as a potentially useful forum for discussion and collective action. But there are lingering doubts about the role of the United States in the organization, the degree to which the hemispheric body represents truly collective interests and not, as was widely perceived in the past, mainly those of the dominant power.

Clearly, one reason for the stagnation and the credibility crisis of the OAS—the feeling that the hemispheric organization was an instrument of the United States in the East-West conflict—is now out of date. Although the OAS still carries for many Latin Americans the negative historical connotation of alignment with Washington, it has been able to confront new challenges and crises largely because it is now free of the ideological straitjacket of the cold war period.[8] Its scope for action has been strengthened by the recent integration of Canada, Guyana, and Belize as full members of the organization; these countries helped dilute the sense of bipolarity between the United States and Latin America.[9] Similarly, the heightened importance of multilateral diplomacy[10] and—in the view of UN secretary-general Boutros Boutros-Ghali—of regional organizations in particular[11] in the post-cold war era have underlined even further the new possibilities for the hemispheric organization.

Moreover, U.S. foreign policy has shifted from the unilateralist approach of the 1980s to multilateralism in the 1990s. Under the Clinton administration, the emphasis on the multilateralist perspective is even more marked than in the Bush years. According to one analyst, a "Clinton Doctrine" of working with partners in international organizations can be perceived in the handling of the Haiti crisis, where the new administration, by "bringing the United Nations and the Organization of American States to the front of the stage," is publicly stating its commitment to solving the problem through multilateral means and working with its "Latin American partners in a newly democratic process."[12]

Does the reemergence of the OAS reflect solely a change in the U.S. approach toward multilateral organizations? Clearly not, since many Latin American countries, having returned to democratic rule, no longer distrust international organizations, feel more comfortable about working in the OAS without the specter of the cold war, and have concluded that a revitalized inter-American forum is necessary to address collectively matters that are of a regional scope. Although some countries may prefer a low-profile and weak OAS so as to deal directly with Washington, most nation-states of the Americas seem to want to preserve a hemispheric forum for collective dialogue between Latin America, the Caribbean, and the United States.

This is not to suggest that the U.S. attitude toward the OAS is irrelevant. The OAS has raised its profile because the United States supported the process of renewal, but also because there was a common purpose among most if not all countries of the Americas to change the hemispheric organization. Of course, the resurgence of the OAS could not have materialized *without* the involvement of the United States— even less so against its will.

The absolute dominance that the U.S. exercised in the OAS during the 1960s has given way to a more balanced situation. As power has diffused throughout the international system at large, with developing countries engaged in more autonomous behavior, so too within the OAS the dynamic of leverage and influence has changed. Nowadays an OAS decision often depends as much on obtaining the consensus of the eleven Latin American countries that make up the core of the Rio Group as on gaining U.S. support. The membership of Canada has altered the "balance of power"; in several instances, Canada has sided with a coalition of South American and Caribbean states to defeat measures supported by the United States and other countries.[13]

Despite the resurgence of the OAS, some critics doubt that it can be truly efficient when decisions must be arrived at by thirty-four active members. The lack of a Security Council mechanism in the organization is viewed as a serious weakness. Such a view, however, ignores the flexibility built into the secretary-general's position. The OAS chief can use his power very effectively, particularly if politically supported by key countries. Moreover, decisions taken by a consensus of all member states, although perhaps less bold than some would prefer, tend to be implemented more resolutely.

The critics are right, though, to point out that even in a changing world, international organizations have enduring defects that limit their potential. Unlike ad hoc multilateral processes, formal organizations like the OAS tend to be slow in reacting to new realities, lack sufficient flexibility, creativity, and focus, and must always take into account that sooner or later, certain initiatives will be stifled by the determined opposition of one or more member states.[14] Therefore, those who favor a more activist OAS need to guard against creating excessive expectations.

Conclusions

B ouncing back from a long period of stagnation and political irrelevance, the Organization of American States is engaged in a process of adapting itself to the post-cold war era. Among the signs of new life are the growing attention of the media to OAS actions; the payment of outstanding contributions to the OAS regular budget by countries—including the United States—in arrears; the accession to full membership status of Canada, Guyana, and Belize; and the creation of new instruments for democratic governance in the Americas.

Most analysts and government officials seem to agree on the utility of a revitalized hemispheric organization to meet the challenges of the new inter-American agenda, the majority of which by their very nature demand a cooperative effort. Moreover, there is a continuing need to have a hemispheric forum where Latin America and the Caribbean can talk over matters affecting the entire area with the United States and Canada. The decline of unilateralism and the ascendancy of multilateral diplomacy in the post-cold war era augurs well for the future of the OAS.

A new common agenda may already be perceived in the work of the OAS, ranging from the promotion of democracy and human rights to the control of drug trafficking and environmental protection. But given the convergence of a long-standing tradition of doctrinal support for representative democracy in the inter-American system with the ascendancy of democratic politics in the region, the process of renewal of the OAS has been characterized by an overriding concern for democratic governance in the Americas. The widely recognized fact that the young democracies are still very frail and that democratic rule cannot be taken for granted has led to an unprecedented effort to deepen and consolidate democratic gains and to discourage and oppose reversals.

Such efforts cause some critics to assert that the American states might end up imposing higher democratic standards and obligations on themselves than the rest of the states in the international community could be held accountable for, thus creating a situation of inequality among equally sovereign states. But it should be noted that the American countries were also much more demanding of themselves in the area of human rights than others at a time when such rights did not enjoy the international acceptance they have today. The record of the period that witnessed the birth of the United Nations shows that the nations of the Western Hemisphere worked hard at San Francisco to insert human rights in the UN Charter and demonstrated international leadership by adopting the American Declaration of Human Rights in 1948, seven months before the Universal Declaration of the Rights of Man was signed in the United Nations. Moreover, the OAS has been attracting renewed public attention precisely to the extent that it has decisively resumed its long-standing doctrinal commitment to promote and defend the exercise of representative democracy,[1] a fundamental component of the Charter that was barely mentioned just a few years ago.

The crises in Haiti and Peru have demonstrated how difficult it is for an international organization to reverse coups d'etat or breakdowns of democratic rule in sovereign countries. Failure to respond effectively to these emergencies could threaten the process of rebuilding of the OAS by recreating an image of incompetence or paralysis. Still, the actions already taken with respect to Haiti, Peru, and Guatemala by the organization, in line with the Santiago Commitment as well as the recent Charter reforms to suspend undemocratic governments, suggest that most countries of the region agree that reacting forcefully against those who would overthrow democratic rule is worth pursuing, even if the desired restoration is not achieved. Such actions could represent something of a deterrent against future conspiracies. At the very least, they would signal a collective will in the Americas to resist the enemies of democracy. In the last analysis, the OAS will be judged by its true ability to act effectively on its doctrinal commitment to the promotion and defense of democracy in the Americas. This will require additional institution building and adequate resources.[2]

As in the case of any international organization, the decisions of the OAS will be most effective when the countries involved are willing to accept assistance or mediation. The OAS is essentially a *political* institution that operates best when it is guided by a criterion of consensus among its member states. To expect the OAS—an organization with a controversial past and constituted by members equal in juridical terms but unequal in size and power—to engage in the use of force to solve a given problem is simply unrealistic. The organization needs to work closely with the United Nations, which has the expertise and the mandate to engage in peacekeeping or peacemaking operations. Following the categories outlined by UN secretary-general Boutros Boutros-Ghali, the OAS is better suited to act in situations that involve electoral observation, preventive diplomacy, and consolidation of peace agreements.[3] In a similar vein, in the area of economic development and technical cooperation, the OAS cannot and should not compete with other specialized regional or subregional organizations like the Economic Commission for Latin America and the Caribbean or the Inter-American Development Bank.

The achievement of relatively modest tasks and well-focused efforts is the recommended road for the OAS as it continues its process of renewal. The organization should concentrate its attention, energies, and financial resources only on a few policy areas of the highest political significance for the member states, setting aside secondary matters or those that duplicate the work of other bodies.

This will require the strengthening of the Secretariat to give it a larger, more politically experienced, and better-qualified staff. According to one view, the OAS is still "a fundamentally weak organization" in terms of personnel; "its governance, leadership, staffing and mandate [must be] substantially strengthened."[4] At the same time, some streamlining in other areas of the organization, such as technical cooperation, will be beneficial. The existing Inter-American Economic and Social Council and the Inter-American Council for Education, Science and Culture, which saw their best times during the Alliance for Progress, could well be combined into a single Inter-American Council for Integral Development, thus saving resources, eliminating duplication, and perhaps also improving the volume and efficiency of technical cooperation.

The process of renovation of the hemispheric organization is far from completed, and its prospects are still uncertain. Many positive changes have occurred, but many more are needed. The international context of relaxation of tensions and the ever-greater intricacy of global ties has helped the process of change, but inevitably the transformations of international organizations tend to lag behind the new realities. Following the often quoted but still valid phrase—recently recalled by the former secretary-general of the United Nations Javier Pérez de Cuellar—the effectiveness of any international organization "depends to a great extent on the political will of its members, including those that unjustly criticize and condemn that organization."[5] If our expectations are not unreasonable about its potential, we may indeed see emerge a new OAS for the new times, an organization that serves the purposes and principles of its Charter and the fundamental aspirations of the people of the Americas.

NOTES

INTRODUCTION

1. See "Pravda Elogia los Acuerdos de la O.E.A.," *El Mercurio*, Santiago, June 11, 1990, p. A1; "Protecting Latin Democracy," *Washington Post*, June 18, 1991; and "Latin Nations Get a Firmer Grip on Their Destiny: Turning to the O.A.S., Not the U.S.A.," *New York Times*, June 9, 1991.

2. See Bernard Aronson, quoted in the *New York Times*, February 7, 1992.

CHAPTER 1

1. See *The Americas in a New World*, report of the Inter-American Dialogue, Washington, D.C., 1990, Chapter 1, pp. 7–9.

2. See "The Santiago Commitment to Democracy and the Renewal of the Inter-American System," AG/doc 2734/91, June 4, 1991; and Resolution 1080, "Representative Democracy," June 5, 1991. The resolution instructs the OAS secretary-general to immediately convoke a meeting of the Permanent Council in the event of any irregular or illegal interruption of the democratic institutional process in any member state, for the purpose of convening, if necessary, an ad hoc meeting of foreign ministers or a special session of the General Assembly that can adopt "any decisions deemed appropriate" within the Charter and international law.

3. See Paul W. Drake, "From Good Men to Good Neighbors: 1912–1932" in *Exporting Democracy: The United States and Latin America*, ed. Abraham Lowenthal (Baltimore: Johns Hopkins University Press, 1991). Drake reminds us that during the period 1914–16, President Woodrow Wilson even sought (unsuccessfully) approval for a Pan-American Liberty Pact in support of republican governments in the hemisphere.

4. See Resolution XXXII of the Ninth American International Conference, Bogotá, Colombia, 1948.

5. According to historian Leslie Bethell, the United States "positively opposed" the efforts of the Caribbean Legion sponsored by José Figueres, Ramón Grau San Martín, Rómulo Betancourt, and Juan Arévalo. See Leslie Bethell, "From the Second World War to the Cold War, 1944–1954," in Lowenthal, *Exporting Democracy*, p. 63.

6. See Resolution No. 837 of the 16th OAS General Assembly in Guatemala, 1986.

7. See Thomas M. Franck "The Emerging Right to Democratic Governance," *American Journal of International Law* 86, no. 1 (January 1992): 46–91.

8. Along the same lines, a proposal originally advanced by Chile was approved to convene a special session of the OAS General Assembly to further amend the Charter so as to restructure and modernize the institutions of technical cooperation for development. This special session was held in Managua in June 1993 and culminated in the approval of reforms updating the OAS institutions for technical cooperation. See AG/doc 11 (XVI-E/92), rev. 1, "Texts Approved by the OAS General Assembly in Its Sixteenth Special Session in Reference to Charter Reforms of the Organization," December 14, 1992.

9. Some of the suggestions outlined henceforth were presented originally in Tom Farer and Heraldo Muñoz, "Reinforcing the Collective Defense of Democracy," paper presented for the Inter-American Dialogue's 1992 plenary session, Washington, D.C., April 1992.

10. See Heraldo Muñoz, "Haiti and Beyond," *Miami Herald*, March 1, 1992, p. 6C.

11. See "Texts Approved by the O.A.S. General Assembly in Its Sixteenth Special Session." The new articles recommend negotiations prior to the suspension of an offending party, a decision that must be approved by a two-thirds vote.

CHAPTER 2

1. The proposal to create this working group was made by Canada, which at the time was only in its second year of full membership in the OAS. The resolution that created the group dealt with general arms control and security matters and was cosponsored by Argentina, Brazil, and Chile.

2. On the CIAV-OAS work in Nicaragua, see "OAS Goes in Peace (That's What It Came for)," *New York Times*, July 16, 1992, p. A12; Santiago Murray, "Building towards Reconciliation," *Americas* 44, no. 3 (March–April 1992): 52–53. See also "Informe del Secretario General sobre los Trabajos y Programas de la CIAV-OEA en Nicaragua," CP/doc 2112/90, add. 2, December 3, 1991.

3. The first OAS civilian monitoring team in Suriname observed the disarmament of warring factions and witnessed, in September 1991, the presidential elections that brought Dr. Ronald Venetiaan to office. On the OAS role in

Suriname, see "Report of the Secretary-General on the O.A.S. Activities in the Peace Process in the Republic of Suriname," CP/doc 2335/93, January 15, 1993.

4. See Heraldo Muñoz, ed., *Environment and Diplomacy in the Americas* (Boulder, Colo.: Lynne Rienner Publishers, 1992).

5. "The Organization of American States and the Issues of Environment and Development," AG/doc 2834/92, May 11, 1992.

6. This working group publishes the monthly bulletin *Initiative*, which contains information about recent developments regarding free trade and economic integration, as well as U.S. congressional activity affecting trade in the Americas.

7. See Abraham Lowenthal, "Mission Encountered: The Organization of American States and the Control of Dangerous Drugs," in Peter H. Smith, ed., *Drug Policy in the Americas* (Boulder, Colo.: Westview Press, 1992), pp. 305–13.

8. The only outstanding issue from the cold war era is the status of Cuba in the OAS. Although Cuba is still a member state, its government continues to be suspended even though the original grounds for the suspension no longer exist.

9. Canada's contribution to the renewal of the OAS has been very significant. Canada advanced the original proposal to create a "Unit for the Promotion of Democracy" and has been particularly active in electoral observation processes, in the Haiti crisis, and in security and environmental initiatives. On Canada's role in the OAS, see Barbara McDougall, "El Compromiso de Canada con la Organización de Estrados Americanos," *Norte-Sur*, June–July 1992, pp. 34–37. Also see Brian J. R. Stevenson, "Entering the Inter-American System: Canada and the O.A.S. in the 1990's," mimeo, Centre for International Relations, Queen's University, Kingston, Ontario, 1991; and Peter McKenna, "Canada in the O.A.S.: Opportunities and Constraints," paper presented to the Canada-Latin American Forum (FOCAL), Washington, D.C., March 1991.

10. According to a 1992 report prepared by the School of Foreign Service of Georgetown University, "multilateral diplomacy will increasingly eclipse bilateral diplomacy." See *The Foreign Service in 2001*, Institute for the Study of Diplomacy report, Georgetown University, Washington, D.C., August 1992, p. 2.

11. See Report of the United Nations Secretary-General, "A Program for Peace," General Assembly/Security Council, A/47/277-S/24111, June 17, 1992.

12. See Howard W. French, "A Clinton Doctrine, Perhaps, to be Tried Out in Haiti," *New York Times*, April 18, 1993.

13. For instance, the vote that approved the presentation of the Inter-American Commission on Human Rights report on Peru at the ad hoc meeting of foreign ministers held in the Bahamas, May 1992, and the December 1992 vote that approved the two-thirds quorum in the Charter reforms to exclude from the organization states in which democratic governments are overthrown through the use of force.

14. On this subject, see Robert B. Andersen, "Unilateralism and Multilateralism in a Transitional World," *Peace and Change* 17, no. 4 (October 1992): 434–57.

CONCLUSIONS

1. See, for example, "O.A.S. Displays New Vitality in Bid to Restore Haiti's Ousted Leader," *Christian Science Monitor*, November 20, 1991, pp. 1–2.

2. This is a view widely shared by external observers and some member states. The effort would involve, for example, the strengthening of the Unit for Democracy promotion as stated earlier. On this subject, see Peter Hakim, "The O.A.S. Feels its Oats," *Hemisfile* 3, no. 6, (November/December 1992). Also see the relevant recommendations contained in *Convergence and Community: The Americas in 1993*, report of the Inter-American Dialogue, Washington, D.C., 1993.

3. Report of the United Nations Secretary-General, "A Program for Peace," op. cit., pp. 6–17.

4. See Richard Feinberg and Peter Hakim, "An Early Test for Clinton," *Christian Science Monitor*, November 24, 1992.

5. Javier Pérez de Cuellar, "Discurso de Incorporación como Miembro fundador del Centro Peruano de Estudios Internacionales (CEPEI) (speech), published by CEPEI, Lima, August 20, 1992.

APPENDIXES

THE SANTIAGO COMMITMENT TO DEMOCRACY AND THE RENEWAL OF THE INTER-AMERICAN SYSTEM

(ADOPTED AT THE THIRD PLENARY SESSION HELD ON JUNE 4, 1991)

The Ministers of Foreign Affairs and Heads of Delegations of the member states of the Organization of American States, meeting in Santiago, Chile, as the representatives of their democratically elected governments to the twenty-first regular session of the General Assembly of the OAS;

Aware that profound international political and economic changes and the end of the cold war open up new opportunities and responsibilities for concerted action by all countries through global and regional organizations, as well as in their bilateral relationships;

Bearing in mind that the changes towards a more open and democratic international system are not completely established, and that therefore, cooperation must be encouraged and strengthened so that those favorable trends may continue;

Recognizing the need to advance decisively towards a just and democratic order based on full respect for international law, the peaceful settlement of disputes, solidarity, and the revitalization of multilateral diplomacy and of international organizations;

Mindful that representative democracy is the form of government of the region and that its effective exercise, consolidation, and improvement are shared priorities;

Reaffirming that the principles enshrined in the OAS Charter and the ideals of peace, democracy, social justice, comprehensive development and solidarity are the permanent foundation of the inter-American system;

Recognizing that cooperation to guarantee the peace and security of the hemisphere is one of the essential purposes consecrated in the Charter of the Organization of American States (OAS), and that the proliferation of arms adversely affects international security and takes resources away from the economic and social development of the peoples of the member states;

Resolved to work for the intensification of the struggle against extreme poverty and the elimination of the economic and social inequalities in each nation and among the nations of the hemisphere;

Noting with interest the report of the consultation group on the renewal of the inter-American system; and

Convinced that the OAS is the political forum for dialogue, understanding, and cooperation among all the countries of the hemisphere, whose potential, enhanced by the admission of new member states, must be increased to make it an effective voice in the world for the decisions of its members,

DECLARE:

Their inescapable commitment to the defense and promotion of representative democracy and human rights in the region, within the framework of respect for the principles of self-determination and nonintervention;

Their firm resolve to stimulate the process of renewal of the Organization of American States, to make it more effective and useful in the application of its guiding principles and for the attainment of it objectives;

Their determination to continue to prepare and develop a relevant agenda for the Organization, in order to respond appropriately to the new challenges and demands in the world and in the region, and their decision to assign special priority on that agenda, during the present decade, to the following actions:

a. Intensifying the common struggle and cooperative action against extreme poverty to help reduce economic and social inequalities in the hemisphere, and thereby strengthen the promotion and consolidation of democracy in the region;

b. Strengthening representative democracy as an expression of the legitimate and free manifestation of the will of the people, always respecting the sovereignty and independence of member states;

c. Promoting the observance and defense of human rights in accordance with the inter-American instruments in force and through the specific existing agencies; and ensuring that no form of discrimination becomes an obstacle to political participation by undervalued or minority ethnic groups;

d. Promoting the progressive liberalization of trade and the expansion of investments, access to scientific and technological knowledge, and the reduction of the foreign debt of the countries of the region and, from this perspective, support for the "Enterprise for the Americas Initiative" and the Uruguay Round of the GATT negotiations;

e. Contributing to the protection of our environment by all for the benefit of present and future generations, thus assuring sustainable development in the region;

f. Encouraging the adoption and execution of appropriate measures to prevent and combat the illicit use and production of narcotic drugs and psychotropic substances, and traffic therein, chemical precursors and money laundering, and related clandestine traffic in arms, ammunitions, and explosives;

g. Favoring integration processes in the region and, to this end, adopting a program of work designed, inter alia, to harmonize legislation in the region, particularly that of the civil and common law systems;

h.   Promoting and intensifying cultural, educational, scientific, and technological exchanges as instruments for integration, with full respect for the cultural heritage of each of the member states;

i.   Increasing technical cooperation and encouraging a transfer of technology to enhance the capabilities for economic growth of the countries of the region.

Their decision to initiate a process of consultation on hemispheric security in light of the new conditions in the region and the world, from an updated and comprehensive perspective of security and disarmament, including the subject of all forms of proliferation of weapons and instruments of mass destruction, so that the largest possible volume of resources may be devoted to the economic and social development of the member states; and an appeal to other competent organizations in the world to join in the efforts of the OAS.

Their decision to adopt efficacious, timely, and expeditious procedures to ensure the promotion and defense of representative democracy, in keeping with the Charter of the Organization of American States.

Consequently, the Ministers of Foreign Affairs and the Heads of Delegation of the member states of the OAS, in the name of their peoples, declare their firm political commitment to the promotion and protection of human rights and representative democracy, as indispensable conditions for the stability, peace, and development of the region, and for the success of the changes and renewal that the inter-American system will require at the threshold of the twenty-first century.

AG/RES. 1080–(XXI–0/91)
REPRESENTATIVE DEMOCRACY

(RESOLUTION ADOPTED AT THE FIFTH PLENARY SESSION, HELD ON JUNE 5, 1991)

WHEREAS:

The Preamble of the Charter of the OAS establishes that representative democracy is an indispensable condition for the stability, peace, and development of the region;

Under the provisions of the Charter, one of the basic purposes of the OAS is to promote and consolidate representative democracy, with due respect for the principle of non-intervention;

Due respect must be accorded to the policies of each member country in regard to the recognition of states and governments;

In view of the widespread existence of democratic governments in the Hemisphere, the principle, enshrined in the Charter, that the solidarity of the American states and the high aims which it pursues require the political organization of those states to be based on effective exercise of representative democracy must be made operative; and

The region still faces serious political, social, and economic problems that may threaten the stability of democratic governments.

THE GENERAL ASSEMBLY RESOLVES:

1. To instruct the Secretary General to call for the immediate
    convocation of a meeting of the Permanent Council in the
    event of any occurrences giving rise to the sudden or irreg-
    ular interruption of the democratic political institutional pro-
    cess or of the legitimate exercise of power by the
    democratically elected government in any of the
    Organization's member states, in order, within the frame-
    work of the Charter, to examine the situation, decide on and
    convene an ad hoc meeting of the Ministers of Foreign
    Affairs, or a special session of the General Assembly, all of
    which must take place within a ten-day period.

2. To state that the purpose of the ad hoc meeting of Ministers
    of Foreign Affairs or the special session of the General
    Assembly shall be to look into the events collectively and
    adopt any decisions deemed appropriate, in accordance with
    the Charter and international law.

3. To instruct the Permanent Council to devise a set of propos-
    als that will serve as incentive to preserve and strengthen
    democratic systems, based on international solidarity and
    cooperation, and to apprise the General Assembly thereof at
    its twenty-second regular session.

DECLARATION OF MANAGUA FOR THE PROMOTION OF DEMOCRACY AND DEVELOPMENT

(ADOPTED AT THE FOURTH PLENARY SESSION, HELD ON JUNE 8, 1993)

The ministers of Foreign Affairs and heads of delegation of the member states of the Organization of American States (OAS), meeting on the occasion of the twenty-third regular session of the OAS General Assembly in Managua, Republic of Nicaragua;

STRESSING that the Organization of American States created at the beginning of this decade valuable mechanisms for the defense of democratic values in the Hemisphere, with due respect for the principle of nonintervention, inspired by the precept that the solidarity of the American states and the high aims which are sought through it require the political organization of those states on the basis of the effective exercise of representative democracy;

RECALLING the important contributions made in this regard by the "Santiago Commitment to Democracy and the Renewal of the Inter-American System", by resolution AG/RES. 1080 (XXI-0/91) "Representative Democracy", by the Declaration of Nassau and by the "Protocol of Washington" on amendments to the Charter of the Organization;

RECOGNIZING that the progress made in defense of democratic institutions must be completed by mechanisms which foster and reinforce democratic government in an integral way, thereby improving its ability to face the challenges of economic, social, and cultural development in all the member states;

AWARE that the Organization has concentrated to a large extent on seeking solutions to crises and that what is needed, in addition, is more effort directed towards preventing such crises;

BEARING IN MIND the part the Organization has been playing in fostering understanding, dialogue, and reconciliation in some member states, with due respect for the principle of nonintervention and the right of peoples to determine their own destiny, as a contribution to strengthening democracy;

CONVINCED that seeking sustainable development has required extraordinary efforts and sacrifice on the part of the developing countries of the Hemisphere, and that more cooperation and external support is urgently needed to ensure that those efforts benefit them with tangible fruits of growth and are not destined to frustrate them for lack of results;

RECOGNIZING the link between improving the quality of life of the American peoples and consolidating democracy;

CONSCIOUS that the ongoing threats to the stability of democratic systems in the Hemisphere call for a new, dynamic, and comprehensive look at the role of the Organization;

CONSIDERING that there is an awareness in the region of the need to improve legal and administrative structures so as to prevent the obstruction of government proceedings that fosters the harmful phenomenon of corruption and discredits authorities and institutions;

REAFFIRMING that the people of the Americas should play a leading role in fighting racism and racial discrimination; and

CONVINCED that no problem facing the member states justifies a breach of the represtative democratic system,

DECLARE:

1. The need to consolidate, as part of the cultural identity of each nation in the Hemisphere, democratic structures and systems which encourage freedom and social justice, safeguard human rights, and favor progress.

2. Their firm belief that democracy, peace, and development are inseparable and indivisible parts of an overhauled and comprehensive view of solidarity in the Americas; and that the ability of the Organization to help preserve and strengthen democratic structures in the region will depend on the implementation of a strategy based on the interdependence and complementarily of those three values.

3. Their conviction that the Organization's mission is not restricted to defending democracy wherever its fundamental values and principles have collapsed, but also calls for ongoing and creative work to consolidate democracy and a continuing effort to prevent and anticipate the very causes of the problems that work against democratic rule.

4. Their certainty that consolidating democracy requires initiatives and programs aimed both at prevention and at encouraging its development, and entails extraordinary efforts to achieve, among other aims, the eradication of the extreme poverty which undermines the full development of democracy among the peoples of the Hemisphere. Therefore calls for the implementation of programs to meet such basic needs as food, health, education, housing, and productive employment, thereby laying the foundations for inter-American cooperation based on the common and solidary goal of integrated development.

5. Their opinion that the support and cooperation provided by the OAS toward strengthening democratic institutions through programs to help the states that request them to enhance their own ability to improve their schemes of political organization goes right to the heart of this new hemispheric commitment. In this regard, they underscore the contribution of the Unit for the Promotion of Democracy and

of the Permanent Council in preparing proposed incentives for the preservation and strengthening of democratic systems in the Hemisphere.

6.   Their conviction that this hemisphere-wide commitment should address the problem of safeguarding human rights with renewed emphasis on the promotion of civil, political, economic, social, and cultural rights. Where violations of human rights are pointed out, educational and promotional activities should also be carried out to prevent situations in which human rights are threatened.

7.   Their support for the processes of modernizing administrative and political structures in those states that request it, in order that governmental action may meet the increasing demands of their people for more effectiveness and more ethical governance.

8.   Their certainty that the strengthening of democratic systems requires in particular cases, efforts to achieve national reconciliation and thereby foster a democratic culture based on the balance and independence of the branches of government, on dialogue and the search for consensus, on respect for the role and responsibility of minorities, and of all political groups and on citizens participation and peaceful political interaction.

9.   Their conviction that all sectors of society in the countries of the Hemisphere must cooperate in a constructive way in strengthening democracy, including governments and political oppositions, and their firm belief that each state should constantly review its public administration with a view to improving governance and the relationship between the government and the governed, in an effort to strengthen democracy, with the cooperation of the OAS, honoring the principle of nonintervention.

10. Their belief that this hemispheric commitment requires that our peoples be given greater opportunity to develop, and that therefore entails closer cooperation founded on a commonality of inter-American interests, genuine interdependence, reciprocal benefits, and the spirit of shared responsibility

requiring that the member states take account of the impact of their actions on development and democratic processes in other member states.

11. Their commitment to continuing and expanding dialogue on hemispheric security among the member states, in a comprehensive and updated approach that takes account of the new international situation with a view to strengthening the peaceful tradition of our Hemisphere and actively contribution to international security and world peace.

12. Their conviction that it is necessary to initiate a broad discussion of the main aspects of integrated development, including bilateral and multilateral financial cooperation, investment and debt, expansion and opening act of intra-regional trade, scientific and technological cooperation, and the environment. Inspired by renewed political will, such a discussion should pave the way for a realistic strategy taking advantage of the consensus reached concerning integrated development.

13. Their reaffirmation of the fact that protection of the environment is fundamental to sustainable development because of its repercussions and effects on the quality of life of people today and its potential for improving the lives of future generations.

14. Their certainty that education plays a vital role in the formation of a new democratic culture of peace and non-violence and that the member states of the Organization will assign high priority to training human resources.

15. Their certainty that trade agreements and especially free trade agreements play an important role in facilitating the growth and consolidation of democracy and, in this regard, their endorsement of the trend towards liberalization and expansion.

16. Their commitment to continue combatting the production, traffic and consumption of drugs and related crimes, among them the smuggling of arms, ammunition and explosives. For this to be successful there will have to be more cooperation

among all the countries of the region and of the wider international community, for the sake of peace within each country.

17. Their appreciation of the valuable work done by the OAS in assisting national reconciliation and the consolidation institutions in some countries of the region. In this context, they note the dynamic role played by the Organization in the country hosting this assembly, where a broad support program, including the ongoing presence of the International Support and Verification Committee, deserves special mention.

18. Their recognition of the importance of technology transfers for development and hence their support for the concept of a Common Market of Knowledge initiative which will allow member states of the OAS to compare notes and exchange ideas in science and technology, given the urgent need to speed up the scientific and technological development of Latin America and the Caribbean, thereby boosting output, broadening opportunities for progress, facilitating sustainable development and enhancing the competitiveness of the economies of the region.

19. Their conviction that an important objective for the strengthening of representative democracy in the Hemisphere is that the armed forces be subordinate to the legitimately constituted civilian authority and that they act within the bounds of the constitution and respect for human rights.

20. This declaration will be called "Declaration of Managua for the Promotion of Democracy and Development."

ORGANIZATIONAL STRUCTURE OF THE OAS

VIRON P. VAKY

The OAS functions through an elaborate administrative infrastructure, described in Article 52 of the Charter:

> The Organization of American States accomplishes its purposes by means of:
>
> a) The General Assembly
>
> b) The Meeting of Consultation of Ministers of Foreign Affairs
>
> c) The Councils
>
> d) The Inter-American Juridical Committee
>
> e) The Inter-American Commission on Human Rights
>
> f) The General Secretariat
>
> g) The Specialized Conferences
>
> h) The Specialized Organizations
>
> There may be established, in addition to those provided for in the Charter . . . such subsidiary organs, agencies and other entities as are considered necessary.

A.   *The General Assembly* is the supreme organ of the OAS and the highest decisionmaking and legislating authority. It holds a regular session annually, either in one of the member states or at headquarters. Sessions are identified sequentially by number. The last annual assembly, for example, was the 23d General Assembly. With the approval of two-thirds of the member states, the Permanent Council may convoke a special session of the General Assembly for specific and special purposes. A special session of the General Assembly on Inter-American Cooperation for Development has been convoked for early 1994. Member states' delegations to the General Assembly are usually headed by their foreign minister.

Among its responsibilities, the General Assembly decides the general policy and action of the OAS; determines the structure and function of its organs; approves the program budget; fixes the quotas of the member governments; establishes measures for coordinating the activities of the various agencies, organs, and entities of the OAS; and generally "considers any matter relating to friendly relations among the American States." (See Chapter XI of the Charter.) Only the General Assembly can approve reforms to the Charter.

B.   *The Meeting of Consultation of Ministers of Foreign Affairs* (frequently referred to simply as Meeting of Foreign Ministers-MFM) is the organ designated to "consider problems of an urgent nature and of common interest to the American States." Any member may request a meeting, such a request being directed to the Permanent Council which decides by an absolute majority vote whether or not to convoke the meeting. Until the foreign ministers can assemble, the Permanent Council is empowered to act as the Provisional Organ of Consultation and may make decisions. Once convoked for a given purpose—for example, Haiti—the meeting is deemed to remain open, like a session of congress, until formally closed by vote. MFMs are usually numbered sequentially as well, but with increasing frequency are labeled "Ad Hoc" if the case is urgent. The meetings convoked pursuant to Resolution 1080 have been called "Ad Hoc"; for example, "Ad Hoc Meeting of Foreign Ministers on Guatemala."

C.   There are three *Councils*: the Permanent Council, the Inter-American Economic and Social Council (CIES), and the Inter-American Council for Education, Science and Culture (CIECC)—although a Charter reform is pending that would merge the last two into an Inter-American Council for Integral Development.

The Permanent Council is in continuous session and is responsible for broad political policies and relations among the states. It is empowered to act as a Provisional Organ of Consultation, and is always the Preparatory Committee of the General Assembly. It is generally the agent for carrying out the decisions of the General

Assembly, except for those matters within the specified competence of the other two councils. The Council is composed of a representative from each member country with the rank of ambassador.

CIES and *CIECC* are responsible for the specialized matters designated in the Charter and indicated by their name. Although the three Councils are technically coequal, the Permanent Council is clearly the "first among equals."

D.   *The Inter-American Juridical Committee*, established by the Charter (Chapter XVII), acts as the advisory body to the OAS on juridical matters and is responsible for promoting the development and codification of international law. The Committee is headquartered in Rio de Janeiro. It is composed of eleven jurists (nationals of the member states) elected by the General Assembly from panels of candidates presented by the members.

E.   *The Inter-American Commission on Human Rights (IACHR)*, also established by the Charter, has the responsibility of promoting the observance and protection of human rights in the region. It also serves as the consultative organ of the OAS on these matters. It is headquartered in Washington, D.C.

Joining the Juridical Committee and the IACHR as a special organ is the *Inter-American Court on Human Rights*. Established by the American Convention on Human Rights, it is an independent judicial organ responsible for applying and interpreting the Convention. It is composed of seven jurists from member states and is located in San Jose, Costa Rica.

F.   *The General Secretariat* is the working arm that carries out the programs and actions decided upon by the General Assembly and the Councils. The Secretary-General directs the General Secretariat and is responsible to the General Assembly for the proper fulfillment of its obligations and functions. The Assistant Secretary-General is the secretary of the Permanent Council.

G.   *The Specialized Conferences* are intergovernmental meetings called to deal with special technical matters or to develop specific aspects of inter-American cooperation. Such conferences have been held in the past on a wide variety of subjects: labor, copyrights, highways, ports and harbors, statistics, telecommunications, natural resources, tourism, and so on.

H.   *The Specialized Organizations* are intergovernmental organizations established by multilateral agreements and have specific functions with respect to technical matters of common interest to the American states. They enjoy full technical autonomy, although they are bound to take into account the recommendations of the General Assembly and the Councils. They submit annual reports on their work, budgets, and expenses to the General Assembly.

There are six Specialized Organizations with headquarters in various cities in the hemisphere. All of them actually antedate the OAS itself:

1.   The Pan American Health Organization (PAHO)—founded in 1902—has as its purpose coordination of efforts to combat disease and general public health matters. PAHO is also the regional agency of the World Health Organization in what amounts to a unique and interesting pattern of relations with the global organization. It is located in Washington, D.C.

2.   The Inter-American Children's Institute (IACI)—founded in 1927—seeks to improve health and living conditions for children. It is located in Montevideo, Uruguay.

3.   The Inter-American Commission of Women (IACW)—founded in 1928—works for the extension of women's rights in the Americas. It is located in Washington, D.C.

4.   The Pan American Institute of Geography and History (PAIGH)—founded in 1928—encourages, coordinates and publicizes geographic, historical, cartographic and geophysical studies of the Americas. It is located in Mexico City.

5.   The Inter-American Indian Institute (IAII)—founded in 1940—is concerned with research for better understanding of and living conditions for indian groups in the region. It is located in Mexico City.

6.   The Inter-American Institute for Cooperation on Agriculture (IICA)—founded in 1942—assists member states in agricultural development. It is located in San Jose, Costa Rica.

I.   Note should be made of *other entities* not determined by the Charter, but which generally collaborate with the organs of the OAS. Notable among these is the *Inter-American Defense Board* (described in the text) and the *Inter-American Statistical Institute* which seeks to improve official and unofficial statistics in the region, and lends technical assistance in this regard.

INDEX

About the Authors

Heraldo Muñoz is currently (since 1990) the Ambassador of Chile to the Organization of American States. He has been a visiting scholar at numerous institutions, including The Brookings Institution, the University of Southern California, and the University of North Carolina at Chapel Hill. He is the author of *Environment and Diplomacy in the Americas* (Lynne Rienner Publishers, 1992) and (with C. Portales) *Elusive Friendship: A Survey of U.S.-Chilean Relations* (Lynne Rienner Publishers, 1991), and is the editor for the "Foreign Relations of Latin America Series" (Westview Press).

Viron P. Vaky was a career officer in the United States Foreign Service for thirty-one years, having served as Senior Member for Latin American Affairs on the National Security Council staff; member of the Department of State Policy Planning Council; U.S. Ambassador to Costa Rica, Colombia, and Venezuela; and Assistant Secretary of State for Inter-American Affairs. He is currently on the adjunct faculty at the School of Foreign Service, Georgetown University, and a member of the Council on Foreign Relations, the Inter-American Dialogue, and the Board of Editors of the *Journal of Inter-American Studies and World Affairs*.